k Sea

Sepik
Manam
NEW GUINEA
Madang
Highlands
Lae
Kukukuku
Port Moresby

Torres Strait

Darwin
Reserve

Reserve

NORTHERN TERRITORY

Townsville

Yendumu
Reserve

QUEENSLAND

Reserve
Alice Springs

WESTERN AUSTRALIA

Central Desert

Ayers Rock

Brisbane

SOUTH AUSTRALIA

Nullabor Desert

NEW SOUTH WALES

Perth

Sydney

AUSTRALIA

Adelaide

Melbourne

THE LAST CANNIBALS

JENS BJERRE

THE LAST
Cannibals

TRANSLATED FROM THE
DANISH BY
ESTRID BANNISTER

WILLIAM MORROW and COMPANY
New York

84617
572.994
B626L

*Set and printed in Great Britain by Tonbridge Printers
Ltd, Peach Hall Works, Tonbridge, Kent*

CONTENTS

Part One

Part Two

With

76

photographic

illustrations

FOREWORD

THANK YOU is an inadequate word for what I feel towards all those who have given me valuable assistance—who in fact made this book possible.

I would like first of all to thank the Australian Government Officials for the many facilities which enabled me to enter restricted areas in Central Australia and in the Territory of New Guinea.

My warm thanks go also to many people, in particular District Service Officers at the various outpost stations, for advice, help and generous hospitality. Without their co-operation my task would have been impossible.

My thoughts also wander back to the brown people whom I learned to love—in the sandy plains of Central Australia, in the rugged mountains and the damp swamplands of New Guinea.

JENS BJERRE

Copenhagen

'No good, Master . . . '

The carrier coolies toiled up and up the mountainside. I urged them to press on more quickly. To encourage them to produce their best speed I had given them small loads and promised them good pay; but after a few days they showed no disposition in the mornings to break camp and get on. I called the boss-boy and asked him what was wrong with the carriers.

'Are they dissatisfied with their loads or with their pay?' I asked.

'No, Master,' he said, 'the pay is enough and the loads are not too heavy.'

'Then what is the matter?'

'Not good go so fast, Master,' he replied. 'Our souls no time to catch up with us. No good, Master.'

PART ONE

1

A Journey Across the Sea: A Stone Age in the Atom Age

THE pitching rhythm of the ship, the steady deep pulse of the engine-room, and the warm wind all help to relax the strain of living in the big city. On the sea one's worries dissolve as they do in an opium dream; time and place have no reality or importance. The sea pervades everything; one's environment ceases to be oppressive. Before long, indeed, one forgets to listen to the ship's radio and leaves unread the daily duplicated newspaper. As the great vessel ploughs along, the past becomes unbelievably distant; the future as unpredictable as the rolling ocean. What is it about the sea that so persistently draws man to itself? Is it some primitive instinct deriving from that time, millions of years back, when life began in some marine protoplasm? An instinct of the same origin as that which brings back birds and fishes across oceanic continents to the place of their birth? All journeys to new and distant countries should be taken by sea. A swift flight in an aeroplane cannot give the traveller that refreshing mental experience which comes from weeks on the water. After a protracted sea voyage the mind is relaxed and the senses receptive to new impressions. A journey on tropical seas, particularly, creates a harmony between man and the physical world: a harmony which promotes a sense of liberation and renewal.

New Guinea was the goal. But the way to New Guinea is by Australia, and I allowed myself a few months in which to satisfy an old and persistent desire to visit the Australian Aborigines. Ever since, in my avid youth, I read Spencer and Gillens' classic book about the weird life and culture of this primitive people, I had longed to see them for myself. So, early one morning, the forty passengers in the pressurized cabin of Trans-Australia Air Lines' large Convair aeroplane roared down the runway of Adelaide's airport, circled the town, and set course towards the North— towards the empty desert. I had begun a journey which would take me the twelve hundred miles to the vast desert of Central Australia. It is not only a journey through space, it is also a journey twenty thousand years back to one of the most primitive peoples in the world, a vanishing race, most of whom live today as they did then. An hour after the take-off we were already over the fringe of the desert. Those passengers who had dropped off for a morning nod now awoke and looked towards the East, where a spectacular sunrise had begun. A red glow moved across the desert throwing long shadows before it. The stars and moon faded away in the growing light, but in the West it was still dark. Even as we looked at this transformation, the sun came through. Below us the desert could be seen in the onset of daylight: a sea of sand through which, occasionally, a rock-formation appeared. Our course lay above one of the outer tentacles of civilization, the railway to Alice Springs, a line which runs through the desert as though it had been drawn by a ruler. To the west lay the barren, sun-drenched Nullabor Desert, which contains the closely-guarded atom establishment at Woomera, where British and Australian scientists are experimenting with the latest type of atomic weapons. A little to the north of them, in the same desert, naked natives sit round a fire making flint knives. Side by side are the two extremes of the process of evolution and human history—the Stone Age and the Atom Age.

Before I began this journey there were many preparations to be made: conferences with specialists in the museums and universities of Australia, consultations with the Government officials in Canberra for permission to enter the Reserve where the native nomads live. Permission to visit them is seldom granted, and the success of my application was due in large measure to the interest of the Royal Geographical Society in London, to Professor A. P. Elkin of Sydney University, and Mr Hergel, the Danish Minister in Sydney.

After seven hours' flight over the drowsy desert, the aeroplane touched down at last at the little town of Alice Springs, which lies in the exact geographical centre of the Australian continent. The moment the door of the air-conditioned cabin was opened, the scorching heat of the desert hit one like the blast from a furnace. After a few days my little expedition was ready. Equipped with a small and sturdy van, supplied by the local agency of the Native Affairs Department, and accompanied by Jimmie, the interpreter, I started off. We disappeared in a cloud of smoke from the exhaust, following a couple of wheel-tracks towards the north-west. It is 250 miles to the last Government Post at Yendumu. Beyond that lies the interminable stretch of bush and rock, and out there was the nomadic tribe I had come to visit. The best distance we could make in a day was little over a hundred miles. At midday the air was so scorching that we crawled under the van, and after these enforced shelters from the heat we tried to make up time by driving far into the night.

On the first night, driving along at our best speed, I suddenly saw an upright figure caught in our headlamps in the sketchy darkness. A moment afterwards there was a heavy bump against the side of the van. Stopping and jumping out we saw what had happened: a kangaroo, blinded by the lamps, had killed itself against the side of the vehicle. This happened two or three times during the journey. We cut off the tails of the dead beasts and grilled them, for they are a great luxury, and left the remainder of the carcass to be devoured by the dingos, the wild dogs of Australia. We slept always in the open. The last time I had done so was in the Kalahari Desert of South West Africa, where we had to keep bonfires going all night to scare away the lions and jackals. In the Australian Desert, where there are no wild animals, we could sleep peacefully.

I enjoyed driving through the desert, for in spite of the immense heat, the vibration, and the sweat that soaks one's body, there is a pleasure in crossing the vast spaces where the horizon is always empty. It is a sensation I enjoyed so much that I started singing at the top of my voice, while Jimmie just grinned. Jimmie and I soon became friends. He gave me some rudimentary lessons in the native language and filled in some of his own background. He belonged to the Wailbri Tribe, the one I was going to visit, and had gone to a mission school where he had learned pidgin-English. He began teaching me a few of the elementary words of his own tongue, a process which I improved on later by my own attendance at the mission school.

On the second afternoon we saw in the distance a group of huts and a windmill.

'Yendumu!' said Jimmie.

The superintendent in charge of this outpost, Mr

Langdon, had been told by radio of my departure and had begun to make arrangements for me to start off a few days later on camel-back. A few of the natives were to be seen in a camp near the mission post: they were all naked, bearded with long hair, and gave a general impression of extreme ferocity. But for all this aggressive appearance, I soon learned to like and respect them.

During my stay at Yendumu, Mr Langdon told me a good deal about these people, as we sat on his veranda in the evenings. The Australian Aborigines are not negroes, they are of Indo-European or Eurasian origin. They are thought to have migrated from Asia to Australia anything from ten to twenty thousand years ago: they have always refused to accept civilization and have withdrawn deeper and deeper into the desert where no white man can survive. When the first Europeans came to Australia there were then estimated to be about 300,000 Aborigines in the country; now there are only about 50,000. Most of these live around the mission stations, but a third of them continue their primitive, nomadic existence in the more inaccessible parts of the desert. They do not cultivate the ground, but are constantly on trek in search of food. They kill animals with wooden spears and boomerangs, and, for the rest, they live largely on snakes, lizards, insects, caterpillars and roots. They get honey from the ant-hills, and from the desert grass they collect seed which they grind and bake into a rough-and-ready bread. They have no huts, but find what shelter they can behind bushes and rocks which protect them against the cold night winds of the desert. In the winter they sleep round fires to keep warm. Men, women and children are all completely naked. Their contact with nature is thus closer than that of any other people in the world, and in this complete isolation they have developed forms of behaviour and belief absolutely different from those of any other race.

On my journey into this strangely preserved primitive world, I experienced many remarkable and incomprehensible things, including some savage ceremonies of witchcraft and exorcism. I learned at last to make some contact with their minds; to find out, for example, that they inhabit a world of imagination very different from ours, so that many of their legends and myths remain quite unintelligible to the white man. They live a life which they have no wish to abandon for anything else in the world. What I had come for was to discover what their values were, what were the sources of their satisfaction and happiness. So my little camel caravan started off from Yendumu towards the west. On the eastern horizon the sun presently appeared, the camels threw long shadows before them and I felt in high spirits as the journey began.

With Mick the camel-'boy' and his grandson Nabi

Adam and Eve, 1954. They sleep under this bush, and in it keep all their possessions—spears, boomerangs, digging-sticks and food bowls

Most of the men are slim and sinewy, and very strong

2

I Eat Caterpillars and Lizards: Mass Hysteria during an Eclipse of the Moon

Animals I like, but not camels. They have no soul, no sympathy with their fellow creatures. They are stubborn beyond all imagination, treacherous and malicious. For several days I sat on the back of one of these fiends, and it seemed to me that the beast swayed as violently as it could from side to side so as to make my ride as insufferable as possible. To start with, one does not feel unduly disturbed by this motion, but gradually, as the muscles of one's back begin to react to the strain, one realizes what the evil intentions of the camel really are. As soon as one gets down, to relieve the anguish by walking, the camel emits an exultant roar. No creature, not even a cockerel, can look so supercilious as a camel through its arrogant half-closed eyes. They have one, and only one, redeeming feature: they can traverse the desert without needing water.

My caravan consisted of three apathetic camels, three natives, the interpreter, Jimmie, the camel driver, Mick, who could also speak a little English, and, finally, his six-year-old grandson, Nabi, who sat interminably on the back of the last of the three camels. We knew that several of the trekking groups of the Wailbri tribe were likely to be found near some rock-formations many miles to the west. The dry season was nearly over, and the only place where they would find water would be in the cracks of the rocks which lay in the shade most of the day. Wherever there is water to be found, the Aborigines are likely to be there. It took us four days to reach this district. Each day towards the evening we tethered the forelegs of the camels and let them browse for what they could get; there was always enough bush and tough desert grass to satisfy their appetites. We slept during the night in the shelter of bushes and rocks. We awoke in a wonderful stillness and the soft light of sunrise, but as soon as the camels rose, the silence was split by their ferocious roaring, the most unmusical sound I have ever heard.

When at last we reached the rocky range we rode along it for some time until we came across the first camping place of the Aborigines. There were in all about thirty or forty of them scattered in small groups at the foot of the cliff. During the time I was with them their numbers changed as families wandered off to find water-holes elsewhere, while others returned from distant travels. When we pitched camp in the late afternoon several of the Aborigines came to meet us, all of them carrying spears. With the assistance of Jimmie and Nick, who knew most of them, I proceeded to make the initial diplomatic contacts. Using the small vocabulary I had picked up from my companions and reinforced by the lessons I had had at the mission school at Yendumu, I began:

'Yandany junu nango!—come here: this is for you.'

I gave each of them some tobacco, which they immediately put into their mouths and began to chew. Jimmie explained to them that I was a friend of his who had come to stay there for some time; and when he added that I would shoot kangaroos for them, they seemed very pleased. Nevertheless, it took several days before all the members of the tribe were reconciled to the presence of a white man and all his strange equipment. The possessions of the men consisted of long spears made out of sharpened branches, small wooden shields, and the inevitable boomerang. The sole domestic equipment of the women consisted of a stick for digging and a few wooden bowls for the collection of food. If they had babies they also owned a few kangaroo hides. But despite this pitiful sum of earthly goods, they seemed to be very happy and contented. Above all, they seemed totally without any inclination to possess or to collect things. One of my first surprises was to find that the children were nearly all blond. Many of them had completely fair hair, even when their eyes and skins were brown. As they grew older, I observed they became darker and darker, and the adults were almost entirely black. It is a phenomenon no doubt derived from their distant Eurasian origin. These natives have never mingled with any other people, and so they have retained their characteristics throughout thousands of years. On the other hand, the natives of the northern shores of Australia have, to some extent, mixed with the Melanesians and do not produce light-haired children any more.

As soon as they realized that my film camera was not a dangerous weapon I had no difficulty in filming them. Indeed, after the first curiosity had worn off, they paid very little attention to me when I was using my camera. During the following seven weeks I went with the men while they hunted kangaroos, wallabies, porcupines and emu, or the large lizards called iguanas, which often grow to more than a yard in length. I went out, too, with the women and children to dig for roots. Their ability to find yams and similar food in this apparently barren land was astonishing. From the roots of one bush they collected fat white caterpillars which were regarded as a special delicacy. These the children would eat at once, raw as they were, but the adults preferred to roast them on the glowing ashes of a fire. As I had not brought a particularly large supply of tinned food, and had already given quite a quantity of it away in presents to the natives, I soon decided to sample the caterpillars and the lizards. The iguana tasted rather like chicken, although the meat had somewhat the consistency of a jelly. The white caterpillars, when roasted, were reminiscent of the crackling of pork. They are often as big as a man's finger, and I found these 'witchity grubs,' of which I have eaten hundreds, truly delicious.

On these wanderings we walked many miles in search of food, and once or twice, failing to get back to the camp by the rocks, we lay down behind the nearest bushes and slept there. I had brought with me a small tent made of parachute nylon, but I never used it for I wanted, as far as possible, to live like the natives. The effort to do so was exacting. The natives ate only in the evening, and on rare occasions in the morning if anything was left over from the night before. I often suffered headaches through hunger and thirst, but these hardships were offset by many memorable experiences.

Some of those nights in the camp I shall never forget. On one occasion we had left camp in company with some of the family groups and gone to a place a dozen miles or so farther west along a rocky range searching for a fresh hunting ground. There were five or six groups, about thirty people in all. The camp was in a ravine of dark red rocks. The evening was still, with no wind stirring and the smoke from the many little fires hung a few feet in the air like a canopy over the camp. Darkness was falling. I had eaten my last tin of bully-beef and lay there idly listening to the sound that arose from the various little groups. There was something particularly soothing in the low susurration of conversation which gradually died down as families went to sleep. Suddenly the quiet was broken by an old man shouting furiously in a non-stop monologue of lamentation. Jimmie explained to me that the man was recapitulating his domestic misfortunes, complaining that two of his wives had left him some time ago and were now living with another man in a distant camp. For two hours or more the old man continued to hold the attention of all his companions. Sometimes there would be loud inter- jections from one group or the other, and from their intonation these comments were evidently expressions of consolation. Gradually, the old man's wailing diminished and finally died away, like a clockwork slowly running down. Even though I did not understand the words I was fascinated by their mood and rhythm. I was told later that these unrestrained expressions of personal grief are habitual among these people, who find in the process a release of nervous tension which prevents the development of what we would call a neurosis. When the pressure becomes too great they simply let off steam in the loud recital of their troubles.

Another night two young men fell into a dispute over a girl. Presently one of them picked up his spear and flung it at the other. The spear pitched a few inches from the first man's feet, upon which he retaliated by doing exactly the same thing. They made aggressive moves towards each other and threw more spears, but always avoided, with great dexterity, an actual hit by mere inches. When they had thus relieved their feelings of animosity, they suddenly ended the mock fight. Tribal life must have its codes of discipline, and these spear-throwing rituals are one method of coping harmlessly with outbursts of anger.

The women had a more drastic method of resolving their differences. One morning two of them began to fight. They stood face to face, each holding a stick. They did not, however, set about each other indiscriminately; they took turns. When one had had a whack she stood quietly for the return blow. My turn. Your turn. And so they went on until one of them gave in and the fight was over.

One evening, some time later, I had an odd experience. I had, as usual, gone to bed early in my sleeping-bag and as the full moon rose and threw its silvery light upon the desert I was gently lulled to sleep by the murmuring of the camp about me. How long I had been asleep I did not know, but I think it must have been about an hour, when I was awakened by the wailing of the women. At first I thought that a fight had broken out among them, but the clamour seemed too general to justify that supposition. I scrambled out of my sleeping-bag, pulled on my trousers, and dashed across to the camp; but even before I got there I realized what was the matter. They were all staring at the moon, which at that moment was just overhead, and there was an eclipse in progress! The shadow of the earth had almost entirely covered the ground. The women were terrified to see the moonlight steadily disappearing and, as it did so, their screams rose to a climax. Some of the men came over looking anxious and chattering fearfully. The women influenced each other with their hysteria and, as the darkness deepened, they fell into a complete panic, running around madly and yelling violently. Jimmie translated for me the most insistent cry:

'Moon him die. Him no more come back. Oh moon——'

The men remained staring upwards towards the place where, a little while ago, they had seen the moon round and shining. They kept on mumbling among themselves but made no attempt to calm the hysteria of the women. By now it was almost completely dark, only the stars showing in the sky. I turned to Jimmie and said in pidgin-English:

'Jimmie you talk along men and women. No be afraid. The moon he come back *lik lik* time. Him come back soon. Me know.'

This message calmed them a little. The men sat down and started talking to each other. The women continued their wailing, though less frenziedly. But only when the moon began to show itself once more, and the light return, did they become reassured. I felt very conscious of the grateful looks they turned upon me as if by magic I had restored the moon. I was a little troubled in case this rare nocturnal experience would be looked upon in retrospect as an evil omen and might be connected with my stay among them. But next day the episode seemed forgotten, although I noticed they watched the moon warily when it came up the following night, and I was relieved when it kept its serene station.

At last my food supplies gave out completely, and so as to help in the housekeeping, I shot kangaroos and wallabies as often as I could find them. The kangaroos always come out to eat just before sunset, and they were relatively easy to hit with a .303 rifle, so long as I was careful to have the setting sun right behind my back. When the animals rose on their hind legs to look in the direction of the noise I inevitably made, they looked right into the sun and were a perfect target. Once or twice on particularly grassy patches, we surprised herds of up to twenty kangaroos at feed. I was often reluctant to shoot as we crept upon them, my companions with spears and I with my rifle. It was a stimulating sight to see the kangaroos leaping across the plain in full flight. I measured the footprints of one specially big animal on its weird progress and found that it covered over ten yards in each bound. Flat out a large kangaroo can work up a speed of twenty-five or thirty miles an hour. If these animals had tried to attack us they would have been a dangerous proposition. When the males fight each other they lash out with their enormously strong hind legs in a kick that would surely kill a man if it landed on him.

Apart from human beings, their only enemies are the dingos, the small desert wolves, who surround the kangaroos and attack them in a pack. From time to time we came across skeletons bleached by the sun that were evidence of desperate battles of this kind. The natives hunt kangaroos, as a rule, with spears and not with boomerangs. The latter they employ against birds and small animals, and a well-handled boomerang can easily cut through the legs of a running ostrich. This weapon is a remarkable example of the inventive skill of primitive man. By his practical sense and keen power of observation he worked out the principle of the aeroplane long before the white man did so. A boomerang is flat underneath and slightly concave on top. When it is thrown horizontally, and rotates in the air, its motion makes the air above the boomerang thinner than the air below, and it is this buoyancy which maintains the boomerang in flight. It is on this same fundamental aerodynamic principle that aeroplanes are made to fly. The Aborigines, who learned so long ago how to exploit the natural laws of the atmosphere, are often described as under-developed, yet for all their primitive characteristics, they have consciously evolved a culture appropriate to their environment.

3

I Become a Member of the Tribe: The Mathematical Marriage System

As the days and weeks went by, I came to feel at home with these desert people, and little by little, to understand something of their way of life. There was no chief to govern the members of each group. There were no rich and poor. The collective responsibility for each little community rested in the hands of its most suitable members: that is to say, the experienced, older men. Their authority, moreover, clearly depended, not upon any inherited right, but upon the confidence the members of the group reposed in them. I was often impressed by the natural dignity of many of these old men and the inner assurance revealed in their bearing and expression, which did not spring from self-pride or a desire to dominate. I have observed a similar demeanour amongst the Himalayan nomads, the Gudjarnes.

The children took a great delight in singing into my portable tape-recorder. When I played the records back for them they sat spellbound by their own voices, and as soon as I stopped the machine they broke into sustained cheers of joy. One lanky girl of about eleven or twelve, called Nanala, was nearly always at my heels, carrying on her hip a baby brother with a very distended belly. She was very bright and showed me how to identify edible roots and how to tell by the foliage of a bush whether there were caterpillars in its roots, and how to divine water at the foot of the cliffs. If my interpreter happened not to be near she explained things with signs and finger-language. One day I bandaged a small boy who had got a long splinter of the hard *mulga* tree into his ankle. The wound gave him great pain when he walked, but no infection set in. (It seemed to me a medical miracle that their numerous cuts and wounds never festered.) In this case I dipped my knife in iodine and dug the splinter out: it must have hurt the little fellow badly, but he never gave a murmur and when the job was finished he stroked my hands to show his gratitude.

I soon became friends with all the children who hung on my arms in clusters when I walked about. I learned their names and took much trouble to pronounce them properly. Their word for me was *djabaldari*, which means uncle. When I was given this name I found myself in the peculiar position of acquiring also two 'fathers' both of them younger than myself. I shall try to explain how this came about, but I warn the reader that he may find the riddle highly confusing to follow.

The rituals of the Australian Aborigines are so involved and obscure that scientists who have studied them for many years are confronted with complicated mathematical conundrums; yet when these are at last solved, they turn out to be unexpectedly logical. The basis of the Aborigines' family system is extraordinary. Before trying to comprehend their patterns of marriage and family relationships, one must exclude from one's mind our own familiar conception of such relationships which are, of course, based upon consanguinity. The fundamental difference is caused by the fact that the Aborigines do not regard

26

children as simply the result of sexual intercourse, but as spirits appearing yet again in a process of reincarnation. Their communities are not made up in our sense of families related by blood, but by groups and sub-groups formally distinguished by the different ways in which they pronounce the names of the individuals within their groups. The child's name is given according to the group or sub-group to which its mother and father belong. Its given-name, moreover, subsequently determines which members of the group or sub-group are possible marriage partners for the children. The syllables of these basic names are capable of numerous arrangements as elaborate as a complicated game of patience. The child's name provides, so to speak, the child's permanent identity disc within the group relationship. When we use the word 'father' we mean our actual parental father. The corresponding word in the Aborigines' language does not, however, signify one man, but several, the others all being members of the group to which the 'real' father belongs. All the members of the main group, similarly, are regarded as brothers though they are not related by blood. The son or daughter of any one of them calls them all 'father'. It is easy to see how there emerge from this habit such paradoxes as that a man may sometimes be older than one of his 'fathers'. Or, similarly, that a child may call his real father, 'uncle'. The same principle applies in all other family relationships. The women of a group can, for instance, be called 'mother' by a child whose actual mother is one of them. When a man marries, his wife's mother does not become his mother-in-law merely in virtue of the marriage. The man marries the daughter of a certain woman because that woman, together with other women in her group, is already his future mother-in-law according to the marriage rules. The nearest possible 'blood' marriage under this system is between half-cousins. A man can only marry a woman of a certain sub-group of the opposite main group and only if, according to her 'rating', it is her 'turn' for his special group. If a man entitled, on this basis, to marry the widow, were to marry her daughter instead, he would be guilty of incest. Again on this basis if a man entitled to marry a certain girl married her widowed mother instead. he, too, would be guilty of incest. The principle whereby each individual in a group is related to all other members of the group creates a unity among them of a most remarkable kind. The primary significance of this system is that each group or family carries prescribed responsibilities. Thus the group as a whole is held responsible for the action of its individual members. From an early age the children are not in the care of their real parents but in the collective custody of the group. For breaches of the law or custom, the whole group, and not the erring individual, is held responsible. If the offence committed is punishable by death, the group does not demand the execution of the real culprit, but is content with the life of any of his group relations.

The Aborigine secures a wife in one of the following three ways: by the distribution of brides on the principle summarized above, or by inheriting a wife of one of his deceased group brothers or, finally, by abduction. The first of these is, of course, the commonest. It proceeds in this fashion. The mother of a small girl decides that she shall be given to a candidate who, according to the pattern of group relationships, has qualified as a son-in-law to the girl's mother. From this moment of decision, even though she is still only a child, she is looked upon as the man's fiancée, until, at the age of twelve or fourteen, she is finally transferred to the husband's keeping. This practice has certain complicated variants. Young newly-married girls can arrange beforehand that their own daughters, when they appear, shall eventually marry a certain man within the group who is entitled to the child on the basis of the relationships I have described. A man may thus find himself in the odd situation of not knowing how many wives he will finally get. Moreover, as the man gets older and gains increasing esteem in the group he is usually given more wives by general consent. So that it is, therefore, quite usual for a man of fifty or sixty to find himself with a wife of fourteen or fifteen as well as his older wives.

It might be inferred, from this practice of polygamy, that there are more women than men among the Aborigines. So far as is known there is little difference between the number of boys and girls born, and polygamy is made possible by the fact that the men seldom marry before they are twenty-five, while the women marry as early as twelve. In considering these matters we should remember that the Christian practice of monogamy, itself relatively new in history, was determined very largely by economic and not religious considerations. Polygamy among the Aborigines, as among other primitive peoples, is the result of the environmental condition in which they live. A woman nursing a small child would find it difficult to collect food in the harsh nomadic conditions of desert life, but if, on the other hand, there are several wives living together, one of them can look after all the children, while the others go out in search of food. Again, a younger wife can look after her husband when he and his earlier wives are too old to find food for themselves. There are, also, manifest disadvantages in this polygamous practice. Many young men of marriageable age cannot find wives because the girls in their group have already been assigned to older men. Youth is naturally drawn to youth, and because of this obstacle many unlawful relationships

29

develop, not to mention outright theft and abduction of wives. I witnessed numerous quarrels and fights because of this. Some of the men are apt to neglect, and even turn out, their old wives in favour of young and fresh ones. In this case the old wives are looked after by their married daughters, but they eke out a very miserable existence. As a rule the wives seem to live in tolerable harmony, but it does sometimes happen that the older, neglected wives get jealous of the younger ones and this, of course, leads to trouble.

As a result of the rule that every widow is automatically transferred to one or more of her husband's brothers, there are no lonely widows or orphan children. Dead men's widows become other men's wives, and are now looked upon as being duly married to these men who, in any case, according to the marriage rules, were always among the possible 'husbands'. The widow's children are absorbed into the other man's family, whom they have always, in any case, called 'father'.

The logical result of these automatic procedures is that no form of marriage ceremony exists among the Aborigines. A girl belongs to her husband as much in her early child-hood as later when he makes her his real wife. These family relationships sound elaborately confusing to us and appear to involve flights into higher mathematics; but ask a little Aborigine about his present and future family identity and he can at once point out and name all uncles, aunts, in-laws and possible wives; further, he can tell the names of all his future children and to whom these will probably be married! Yet there are people who believe, because the Aborigines are physically under-developed, that they are also mentally backward.

4

Bloody Ceremonies in the Desert: Native Love Life

ALMOST every night I used to sit for an hour with Jimmie, the interpreter, surrounded by the old men of the tribe. I tried to tell them, in simple metaphorical language, a little of the world beyond them, but I think they found it all beyond their range of imagination. They could not conceive, for example, that water, which to them is so rare and precious, could exist in such great volume as a lake or ocean across which it was impossible to see the other side. But these conversations led them to tell me something of their own remote life, of their legends and myths, their notions about life and its origin. The women were always sent away from the camp-fires when these confidences began, and I was told that if a woman should ever eavesdrop on the men's private rituals, she would be killed at once.

One evening some strangers returned to the camp with the men, who had been out hunting. They brought with them a twelve-year-old boy who was going through various initiation ceremonies and had, together with some of his nearest male relatives, been on a pilgrimage to secret holy places, where certain spirits lived. Now the boy had come back to be circumcised, the first important event in his

passage from childhood to manhood. The old man con-
sented to let me witness the ceremonies about to take
place, which only very few white people have ever witnessed. The initiation ceremonies, which often last several
weeks, mark the change from happy, carefree childhood
to disciplined manhood, from irresponsibility to responsibility, from ignorance to knowledge. It is a drastic change
for the boy who goes through it; he enters a completely
new world of spells and incantations from which he learns
his basic tribal lessons: how the world was created, the
history of the tribe, the religion and ethics of his people.
He undergoes painful inflictions, the memory of which
teaches him not to forget what he has learned.

What I experienced the next few days both shocked me
and moved me. The day the circumcision took place, I
went with all the men and the boy-candidate to one of
their holy places a few miles away. It was a bare, sandy
spot, surrounded by *mulga* trees and salt bushes, a sanctuary
which the women were always careful to avoid. The men
sat down in a circle and started to chant in a monotonous
rhythm, beating time on the ground with their boomerangs.
It was not an exciting rhythm; but its persistence produced
an hypnotic effect. The same cadence was repeated over
and over again, beginning on a high piercing note and
slowly fading like waves breaking in the surf and then
rolling heavily up on the beach.

The oldest of the men did not take part in the chanting,
but lay by themselves in a small group stretched out as if
asleep. The boy lay between two of the old men, his head
upon the ground and away from the singing men. He had
been subjected to this softening-up rhythm for several
sessions already and was now in a state of relaxed but
receptive torpor. The psychological effect of this insistent
chant, which went on for several hours, rising and falling

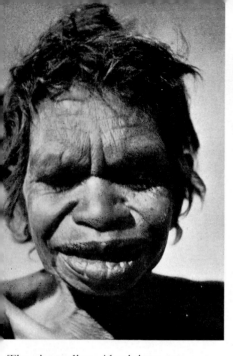

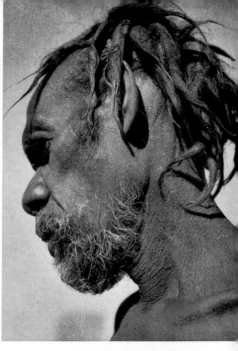

The Australian Aborigines are
of Eurasian origin. Few have
thick lips like this woman

The men often rub fat into their
hair. This man's ears are particularly high

The Stone Age in the Atomic Age. Fashioning knives out of flints

Collecting precious rainwater from clefts in the rocks

I gradually made friends with the aborigines and began to understand their way of life

and accentuated by the beating of boomerangs on the ground, became more and more emphatic; the very air was possessed by the vibration. Whatever the meaning of the words, the purpose of the chant was to stamp them permanently upon the boy's mind.

Suddenly the song stopped. One of the men in the circle gave a sign, on which the others rose and took up prescribed places. Two of them got down next to each other, on hands and knees. Two others took the boy by his arms and legs and slung him upon the back of the two kneeling men; and two or three other men came forward to hold the boy in position, face upwards. A stick was put between his teeth for him to bite on. One of the boy's uncles, old Minjena, now joined them and with a sharp flint bent over the boy and performed the circumcision. It lasted only a minute or two, but I realized afterwards that I was biting my lips and clenching my hands to control myself. I could see the boy held down on the human 'operating table', his body trembling with pain and tension. Under the blazing sun everything was still except for the cooing of a distant desert pigeon.

Finally, the man stood aside and helped the boy to his feet. He stood there, blood dripping from him; then he walked slowly across to the old men who, for the first time during the ceremony, raised themselves from the ground. They stared a whole minute at the boy, without saying anything, then lay down again. The rest of the men now resumed their rhythmic chant and beat the earth with their boomerangs. The boy was now taken a little way off, where he squatted over a small, smoking fire, covered with leaves, and kept his position there for nearly an hour, no doubt to cleanse and disinfect the wound. His face was apathetic and expressionless; no one spoke to him, but the chant was kept up for a long time.

A few days later I witnessed further stages of these grim
initiation ceremonies, held in another sacred spot. While
some of the men sat in a circle and sang, others went
behind some bushes. I followed them and saw that some
of the biggest and strongest of them were opening a big
vein in their arms with a pointed flint and causing the
stream of blood from these gashes to spurt over the
novitiates so that it ran in stripes down their bodies. Blood
is the source of strength, and by thus drenching the young
boys with their mature blood, the men were giving them
the fortitude to endure the rites of manhood. Afterwards
they decorated themselves in various ways with white
ashes, black charcoal and branches and performed a vivid
dance, in which they impersonated dingos attacking a
kangaroo.

Finally, in the early evening, before darkness fell, they
performed the final initiation on a youth of fifteen or
sixteen. He knew what was about to happen, and putting
a stick between his teeth, so as to grind his pain into
silence, he lay down on his back on top of two men, who
as before were kneeling down to furnish an improvised
operating table. What followed is difficult to describe
outside a medical gathering. With a sharp knife they
performed a deep operation which, without depriving the
young man of his power of propagation, yet regulated the
use of it to special occasions. A hole was pierced right
through his sex organ near the root, and there was inserted
into it, at either end, a splinter to keep the aperture from
growing together again. The object was to ensure that
henceforth the urine and the sperm would be ejected
through this little hole high up on the sex organ, instead
of by the normal channel. Only when the lad put a finger
on the hole, and kept it there, would the fluids in future
be able to pass through the proper outlet. The boy did

not utter a sound while this grisly operation was performed, and only with difficulty could he stand on his feet afterwards. His body trembled, he glistened with sweat, his eyes were glazed with silent agony.

This grotesque and revolting practice has an obvious explanation. The Australian Aborigines are probably the first primitive people to devise a wholly effective birth control. In the baking wilderness they inhabit, numbers must be kept down, for they cannot maintain large families on their low level of subsistence; and long treks would be impossible with a large family of small children and babies in arms.

The initiation of girls is trivial in comparison, and consists of cutting tribal signs on the upper part of the body—as a rule some long scars across the breast—immediately after the first sign of maturity. The other preparation for womanhood is a rough-and-ready puncture to prepare her for mating with men. The puncture is performed by an old man belonging to the girl's family group, assisted by an old woman whose role is to pacify the girl while the crude deflorescence is accomplished. The only concession made to the weaker sex is that the old man winds some kangaroo hairs round his finger so as to carry out his job as gently as possible.

Afterwards the men who happen to be present and who, according to the marriage laws, are eligible as husbands have intercourse with the girl. If she is not already promised to one of them, she continues to have casual intercourse with men of her group until she gets married. Even after marriage it sometimes happens at special ceremonies that she is 'lent' to one of the other unmarried men who, by group rules, might have become her legal husband. A man who objects to lending his wife in this way to a tribal brother on a visit is considered greedy and anti-social.

35

The notion is widespread that primitive people live a life of sexual excess. While it is obvious that their morality differs widely from ours, the fact remains that theirs, too, is governed by principles of behaviour determined by their beliefs and environment. The naked natives in the desert do not look upon sexuality as something to be concealed in the presence of others. They regard it as something normal and necessary in life and they speak freely about it, even when children are present. They have virtually no private lives. Intimacy between the sexes never occurs during the night but always in the day-time, and the only semblance of privacy about it is that it occurs as a rule a little away from the others and in the shelter of a bush. Both men and women make use of various love tokens. The man offers the woman he seeks to inveigle, meat or berries, which he claims to have 'charmed'. The woman's armoury of methods also includes a repertory of ingratiating songs which she croons to the man of her choice until he succumbs to her insistence.

Young married women often run away with a lover, and if the lover belongs to the right group and is thus in the category of hypothetical husbands, no serious social offence is involved. But if he is not in the proper group, the elopement is regarded as a serious and punishable offence. The husband's relatives will pursue him and wound him with spears. If, on the other hand, the eloper is within the right marriageable group, the husband alone chases and fights with him—and the woman becomes the prize of the victor. If the husband wins she gets a beating into the bargain. Such duels are generally fought with heavy sticks and, as a rule, neither of the men is mortally wounded. Most of the wayward wives appear sooner or later to return to their husbands. In spite of these irregularities, and although the wives are often brutally treated, there is abundant evidence among the Aborigines of real affection and marital harmony, especially among the older couples. I often saw some of the older women quietly staring for hours on end into the desert in the direction from which they expected their husbands to return from hunting.

In some of their tribal ceremonies the Aborigines sing very candid love-songs, which leave little to the imagination; and I once watched some young girls performing a very provocative love-dance with such guilelessness as to enhance their natural charm. To them love-making is an elaborate game. They do not believe that pregnancy is solely the result of intercourse. It is said that a missionary, anxious to arrest the falling birth-rate among the natives, proposed that they should sleep more often with their wives. The men, however, claimed that the reason why they did not get so many children nowadays was because they were too preoccupied with the white man and all the new and perplexing situations he brought with him. His presence worried them so that they lost their mental and spiritual equilibrium, and were thus not able to get the right dreams for producing children. They believe that pregnancy itself originates in dreams. First, by sexual intercourse, they make the physical substance of the child; subsequently they create its soul through a dream. In the dream the father's soul wanders about the countryside and at some spot, generally near the water-hole from which his own soul originates, he meets a so-called 'spirit child'. After he has dreamed of his spirit child he passes its image on to his wife in another dream. Without these dreams, they say, a woman cannot become pregnant.

It is, indeed, a fact that the birth-rate has fallen considerably in the places where the white man has intruded on their territory, even when his presence has not brought the usual diseases of civilization, nor in other

37

ways affected the natives' style and standard of living. It may well be that the presence of white men has a pervasive effect on aboriginal psychology, even to the point of affecting pregnancies. Our own medical profession is familiar with the type of woman who does not become pregnant till she has adopted a child and, in that way, psychologically disposed herself to motherhood.

5

The Ceremony of the Holy Snake: The Medicine-men in a Trance: The Miracle in the Desert

IT was towards the end of the dry season and my stay with the tribe was drawing to an end. My three 'stabled' camels consumed so much water that the women by now had to go far up the mountainside to find enough for them, and they came down bearing it in wooden bowls covered with grass so as not to waste a drop, either by evaporation or by spilling. I had only a few more rolls of film left, and no stores at all. I was beginning to think of departing, when Jimmie came to me one day and told me that the old men had decided that I could go with them to Ngama. He seemed very impressed by the offer, and I gathered from him that Ngama was one of their most sacred places. Jimmie would not himself tell me what Ngama was, for he was not initiated in its rites, so he took me along to one of the old men who was already particularly friendly towards me. I could never pronounce his name and so I called him Bob, a name which seemed to please him considerably. Bob told me, through Jimmie as translator, that Ngama was the Great Snake, which long ago had created the entire world, the mountains, the desert and all. Its spirit dwelt under a large rock farther out in the desert, and the whole region around it was sacred.

We started early next morning towards the south-west, accompanied only by fully-grown men who had reached a certain age and maturity. Four of them had never before visited the shrine and were to be initiated into its mysteries on this occasion, thus achieving their full and final tribal status. About midday we came to the rock which lay on a flat piece of desert, surrounded by salt bushes and tough desert grass. It was of sandstone about ten to fifteen yards high and about a hundred yards in circumference. The four men to be initiated left us and went off by themselves to the other side of the rock. As we drew nearer I could make out a huge painting on the face of the rock which leaned outwards and was protected by overhanging cliff formations. The picture represented a huge snake winding itself along the face of the cliff. It was fifteen or twenty yards long and painted in black, red and white charcoal, ochre and chalk, no doubt mixed with plant juice. The painting looked old, and I learned later that it had been preserved from generation to generation, possibly for thousands of years, and that the colours had been freshened up from time to time.

One of the old men, Djinbanada, went alone to the head of the snake while the rest of us kept a little distance away. The old man was highly esteemed in the tribe, and was indeed the guardian of the rock, which no one was allowed to approach unless accompanied by him. He now proceeded to address the Spirit of the Snake. Facing the rock, which arched towards him, he shouted several times in a loud and vibrating call produced by clapping one hand over his mouth. The cry was thrown back in a strong and distant echo. Having thus wakened the spirit of the Snake he signalled for the rest of us to come up. Three or four of the oldest men bent down and, with Djinbanada, pulled from a secret hollow in the rock an oval moulded

Male kangaroos fight with
their powerful hind legs

Nanala digging for yams

Looking-out for kangaroos

Nearly all the children are blonde, but become dark as they grow
older. This is Nanala

The strongest men in the tribe pour their blood over the boys to give
them strength for the hardships to come

They walked slowly past the rock-drawing of the Snake, while
Djinbanada explained its legend

The men sat in a circle and sang in a monotonous rhythm; they wer
not disturbed by my tape-recorder

stone on which were engraved a number of circular designs. These emblems, sometimes made of wood, are called *tjurunga*. The old men very gently touched the inscriptions with their fingers devoutly murmuring as they did so. Their whole attitude expressed deep veneration. The inscriptions on the stone recorded the history of the tribe from its supposed origins, and the veritable spirit of the tribe is believed to inhabit the stone and to endow it with an immemorial magic. Generations come and go, but their unity as a tribe is miraculously embodied in the sacred stone. This act of worship and belief seemed to me something infinitely beautiful and exalted; it was animated by a devotion as deep as any I have experienced in church or temple.

I should have liked to bring my camera right up to the *tjurunga*, but I felt that such an act would be offensive and disruptive, so I remained at a distance with the others until the old men had again concealed the *tjurunga* at the base of the rock. As if old Bob had read my thoughts he now nodded imperceptibly to me and, with the others, I went forward to the rock.

The four men to be initiated, and who had remained behind the rock all the time, were now summoned. They walked slowly in a row headed by the old men along the whole length of the Snake design from head to tail, each man tracing the design with one hand as they went.

On either side of the Snake I could now see painted signs, each one representing scenes of desert life; a sand-hill, a rock, a water-hole, a dried-up salt lake. As the men slowly moved past the painting, old Djinbanada narrated its history and meaning: how the Snake had created their country long ago in the dream world when the universe was young. The initiates repeated his narrative a sentence at a time, so as to impress it upon their minds and be able to pass the legend on to the next generation. The ceremony ended with all the men sitting in a circle, singing and beating time on the ground with their boomerangs.

Night had fallen before we reached the camp, for we walked slowly, as some of the old men found difficulty in keeping up. It was the middle of the winter when it can sometimes get bitterly cold during the night. On the way home, therefore, most of the men carried a piece of burning *mulga* wood in their hands, and while they walked they swung the burning wood around them, in order to keep warm. By manipulating the wood in a certain way they could keep it constantly alight, but when I tried to imitate their action I could keep my own torch alight for barely a minute. It amused them to watch my clumsy attempts to do something which for them was the most natural thing in the world.

Aborigines are inclined to look upon misfortunes and accidents as induced by magic, and they turn therefore to the tribe's medicine-man for coping with the magic. If, for instance, a group has been unlucky on its hunting excursions for several days running, and has failed to bring any food home to the camp, they conclude that they are the victims of an evil spirit. You can sense the deep depression which comes over them all. Then the medicine-man is summoned; he gathers the men around him and makes them sit all night singing incantations which are designed to ward off the evil spirit. The chants of the medicine-man seem gradually to hypnotize the men into a mood of optimism and self-assurance, and presently the medicine-man declares that the curse which the evil spirit laid upon the group has been dispersed. In one way he is right; the collective mood of depression has been dissolved.

The medicine-man is not a witch-doctor so much as a spiritual guide and pastor to the tribe. If he loses his influence on them, the tribe is in danger of dissolution and decay. A medicine-man must not only be endowed with a strong personality and a dominant mind; tradition demands also that he must have undergone special spiritual revelations in order to assume his role. He must be able to send his spirit across long distances to gather a variety of experiences which then become embodied in his subconscious mind and are transmuted into the visions which he discloses in a state of trance. His distinction is that he possesses what our psychologists call remote perception. Even ordinary dreams the Aborigine regards as visions which the soul has seen on the journeys it makes during physical sleep.

For a man to be accepted as a medicine-man his dreams and spiritual experiences must be of a special visionary quality, and he must have, above all, hypnotic and telepathic powers of communication. He dreams many dreams and sees many visions before he finally achieves that singularity of spiritual experience which qualifies him as a medicine-man. Before he can secure the faith and confidence of the tribe the medicine-man must have fulfilled some profound mystical experience. This he might achieve by hypnotizing himself into a trance during which potent spiritual powers might possess him. The trance might continue for several days; indeed, the longer the better. In it the dreamer might find himself returning to the element from which man first came—water; and as he sinks back into the elemental water he meets the origin of life, the legendary holy snake, who confers upon him the precious spiritual powers which he needs to become a medicine-man.

Another acceptable spiritual experience which could

qualify him as a medicine-man is described by the natives in the following fashion:

The soul of the man destined to become a medicine-man leaves his body, upon which he falls into a profound slumber. No one dares to wake him, even if the sleep should continue for several days. The soul goes voyaging to those distant places from which it originally came; and there, in a brightly-lit cave, it encounters two snakes, who constantly divide themselves and create new 'spirit' children. Many of these newly-fashioned spirits unite in a mystic communion with the soul of the dreamer, giving him a spiritual strength far exceeding that of an ordinary man. When the dreamer wakes up from his trance he relates these experiences to the tribesmen, and if they are sufficiently impressed he is appointed, so to speak, a probationary medicine-man and takes lessons from the older medicine-men who teach him the full routine of their craft. When the medicine-man tells of his strange experiences in the trance he does not differentiate physical from spiritual reality. What the soul did while the body lay in its torpor is something which, in the fullest sense, *happened* to him. For the Aborigine there is no distinction between dream and reality, so that one can almost say they live in another dimension from ours.

Outstanding medicine-men, they say, are rarer among the tribes nowadays because the spiritual atmosphere has been disturbed by the presence of the white man. In the old days the medicine-men enjoyed an assurance which enabled them to account for all phenomena; they had an explanation for everything. But the invasion of their lives by the values of civilization upsets their primitive balance, and they cannot concentrate on their own world. It seems impossible for the younger generation to attain that intense concentration of sensitivity which makes a good medicine-man. They do not 'dream' so deeply; their dream-world is no longer so fully integrated with their physical world. The whole psychological balance of their outlook is disturbed.

Many scientists have sought to penetrate the mystery of the medicine-man. The anthropological faculty at Sydney University has frequently sent ethnologists and psychologists to Central and Northern Australia to study the phenomena of the medicine-man's activities. Professor A. P. Elkin, Australia's leading specialist on native cults, believes that medicine-men have developed an abnormal sensitivity or perception which amounts to a sixth sense. He repeatedly observed that the medicine-man in a trance was able to tell in minute detail what some of the tribe were at that moment doing *on the other side of a hill*. The scientists could observe these phenomena, and describe them in appropriate terms, but they could not explain them. The medicine-man himself had a simple explanation: his spirit had left him, visited the tribesmen on the other side of the hill and noted what they were doing!

A few days before I was due to start back to Yendumu old Bob came to me with something hidden in a piece of kangaroo skin. Out of the skin he produced an oval piece of wood with circular designs on it—a *tjurunga*. He gave me to understand that it was for me alone, and that I must not show it to anyone in the tribe and most especially not to the women. It was very old. It had been given to him by his father, when he was a boy, and was a 'dream story', as Jimmie told me, of something that had occurred very long ago. I was greatly moved by the gift. In the morning, two days later, when I was packing for Yendumu, old Bob came to me and asked if he might borrow the *tjurunga*. I gave it back to him still wrapped in the skin, and he disappeared with it behind some salt bushes. A few hours later, the camels packed and all ready for departure, I walked over to the salt bushes to look for old Bob. There sat my friend, staring at the *tjurunga*, the tears running down his cheeks. I signed to him that he could keep it, but he pressed it firmly into my hands. The *tjurunga* is now with me in my home. That it was given to me by Bob makes it more precious to me than all the medals and decorations in the world; it reminds me of experiences I shall never forget; of days and nights with those fascinating people in the far-off desert.

*　　*　　*

What is Ayers Rock? It is a natural phenomenon, which has been seen by few white people. Yet in its grandeur and beauty it compares with such other wonders of the world as the Victoria Falls or the Grand Canyon. It is a huge, compact rock, which stands 1,600 feet high in the wastes of the Central Australian desert. It is two miles in diameter, about eight miles in circumference, and changes colour to violet from red as the sun catches it from various angles. It is the world's biggest stone. The nearest habitation is the little desert town of Alice Springs, 300 miles to the north-east. Beside Ayers Rock is the greatest sanctuary of the Central Australian Aborigines called Uluru; and the neighbouring area is a reserved territory for the Pitjendadjara tribe, which no white man may enter without a permit from the Government. When I returned to Alice Springs from the Yendumu Reserve, I met two American anthropologists just starting to Ayers Rock to study the rock paintings. I joined them, and we secured permission from the Native Affairs Department to stay in the Reserve for eighteen days.

We left in a van with food and water, enough for three weeks. For four days we drove through a varied landscape of scorched desert grass, cliffs and ravines, twisted *mulga* trees, desert oaks, and salt bushes; across red sand-dunes and dried-up salt lakes, where the wheels powdered the white crust. The days were hot and the nights bitterly cold; it was winter now, but we slept snug in our American sleeping-bags. Day after day we spent many hours man-handling the van through bad patches, but we kept moving on and finally reached Ayers Rock.

We saw it first, from the top of a sand-dune, like a red marble dome on a vast yellow carpet. Then it disappeared from sight as we pressed on through the sand-dunes. Later it came into sight again for a whole hour, gradually becoming bigger as we drew nearer. At one point, which we guessed was only about three miles away, we found we were actually twelve miles from the Rock, so confusing is the judgment of distances in the desert. Around it grew comparatively large trees, which drew their nourishment from the rainwater draining from the Rock. At last we arrived. The red granite walls arose almost perpendicular from the desert; and at close quarters this enormous monolith was like a natural cathedral, overwhelming and majestic. I felt the same excitement as when, a few years ago, I saw the thunderous power of the Victoria Falls or my first sunrise on Himalayan peaks.

We made camp in one of the high, deep caves which fierce sandstorms, through the centuries, have worn in the sides of the cliffs. As it happened, the first night we were there, one of these violent whirlwinds blew up, a warning that the rainy season was near—and much earlier than usual. Next day we had the first thunderstorm. It did not rain in the usual way; the clouds just fell down in large lumps. The water cascaded down the sides of the Rock, and in a very short time a river was roaring outside our cave. I could understand how it was that so many soldiers had been drowned during the last war, in rainstorms in the Sahara. Ayers Rock now lay like an island in the ocean. We could have saved ourselves the trouble of bringing along in the lorry our forty-gallon cask of drinking water. For four days we had several more sudden thunderstorms and whirlwinds; and as we were stormbound in our cave we had plenty of time and opportunity to study the native rock-paintings on the walls and roof of the cave, painted, perhaps, thousands of years ago. There were symbolic designs by the score, and vivid depictions of hunting scenes, too. While the rain lasted we discussed primitive art. One of the Americans thought that a primitive man draws an animal, such as a kangaroo, in order to exercise some power of magic over the animal and thus make sure of killing it during the hunt. The other American preferred to think that the motive of the Aboriginal artist was simply the spontaneous desire of every child of nature to draw. There is doubtless something in both theories.

Suddenly the rain stopped. The torrents of water around the Rock disappeared with astonishing speed, sank into the sand or evaporated in the burning sun. Not until now had we really had a chance to examine the Rock. It was only possible to reach the top in one place, and it took two concentrated hours, with many halts on the way, to climb it. In several places there were such sharp angles that we had to pull ourselves up by our fingers and toes from crack to crack. We were rewarded at last by an enchanting view across the wide desert to the far horizon. Up here, on the roof of the Rock, were innumerable water-holes worn by the rain through the ages.

A few days later we made a complete circuit of the Rock. On all sides the wind and the tempests had worn deep caves in the granite, and in most of the caves the walls were decorated with paintings. Far up the sides there were more caves, some big enough to hold a church. In other places the weather had peeled off the rock-face and left deep cracks of fantastic shapes. In one spot the weathering had produced an enormous skull, which glared across the desert; and to make the similitude still more grotesque, the cranium was inhabited by birds of prey— hawks and eagles. In the lesser caves were flocks of rock pigeons and ravens.

Ayers Rock was most beautiful at sunset, when the colours changed every minute in a sequence of blood-red, purple, burgundy and violet. When the sun was half-way down, the shadow of the Rock was thrown far out towards the opposite horizon. During the night, the light of the moon and the stars produced even more fantastic patterns, while from the caves came the weird cries of the wild birds—or was it the tumultuous voice of Uluru, the spirit of the rocks?

PART TWO

6

New Guinea—The World's Most Unapproachable Island: By Helicopter to the Primitive Past

IT is a long jump from the jungle of Australia to the jungle of New Guinea; yet it is only from one Stone Age to another, from desert nomads to cannibals. After the hardships of the Australian desert I rested for a week or so with the Danish Consul, Mr Horn, in Townsville, on the east coast of Australia; and then set off one morning in a four-engine triple-decked Qantas seaplane straight across the Coral Sea and the Torres Straight to Port Moresby, the largest town on the south coast of New Guinea. New Guinea has been known for more than four hundred years; but it will be many years yet before the last cannibal there has finished his favourite meal. Hundreds of thousands of its people still do not know of the existence of the white man. It remains the least explored part of the inhabited world.

It has been said of New Guinea that God created the island on a Saturday night, just before closing-time. He had to hurry, so that, after finishing its outline, he hurriedly flung the rest together in a mad confusion of mountains, swamps and rivers. Some parts of it are called 'broken-bottle country' by airmen because, from the air, the craggy chalk cliffs look like a heap of broken bottles. In proportion to its size, New Guinea has more mountains than any other island in the world. If God had not been so pressed He could easily have made it the largest island in the world, instead of the second largest, by merely unravelling some of the mountain ranges; anyone who has explored its interior must wish that He had done so. In a day's march one can advance only a few miles as the crow flies; the tracks, when they exist, coil and twist up and down steep mountain sides. There is always a canopy of cloud over the mountain tops, as if the earth had not yet cooled off after its creation; and, indeed, New Guinea has not cooled off, for there are several active volcanoes on the island, one of which, Mount Lammington, erupted a few years ago and killed at least 3,000 natives.

In 1511 a Portuguese sailor, Antonio d'Abreuva, landed on the beach of New Guinea but soon left the inhospitable island and its savage tribes. One of his compatriots, Jorges de Menezes, gave the island its name when he touched there a few years later; but the first man to show a sustained interest in New Guinea was the Spanish adventurer, Torres, who seized the island for Spain in 1606. The Spaniards, however, made little impression on the island, for the savage tribesmen made colonization impossible. A hundred and fifty years later the British, through the East India Company, laid claim to the island but they, too, did not show an active interest in their new possession and did not even protest when the Dutch in 1828 seized the western half of the island and incorporated it in the Dutch East Indies.

None of these successive occupying powers showed a disposition to pacify the wild cannibals until Germany, in 1884, seized the north-east part of New Guinea along with the group of islands in the Bismarck Strait. About the same time, the British set up a protectorate over Papua, the southern part of the island. This parcelling out of

New Guinea amounted to little more than putting different colours on the map, and even up to the first World War only a few colonists dared to penetrate the hill country more than a few miles from the coastal settlements. The climate, the mountains and the bloodthirsty tribes combined to protect the seclusion of the island. After the first war the Germans were thrown out and the Australians took over the eastern half of New Guinea, under a mandate from the League of Nations, now the United Nations. In the years between the two wars some progress was made in developing the country: gold and oil were found there, saw-mills were built and coconut groves were planted. But this development was very limited; the Europeans still kept to the coast towns; there were no roads into the interior. As late as 1940 seven-tenths of New Guinea was unknown territory.

It is difficult to estimate the population of New Guinea, but it lies somewhere between one and two million. There still exist, high in the wild Karius Mountains, unexplored, isolated valleys—Shangri-Las—peopled by elusive, undiscovered tribes. As late as June, 1954, an Australian flyer, off course, found a hidden valley containing about 100,000 people. New Guinea is a fantastic island. The climate on the coast and in the river swamps is a purgatory of mosquitoes, malaria and humid, stifling heat. In the mountains it is still clammy and wet, but at least cool. Every single day, all the year round, it rains somewhere along the coast or in the mountains. New Guinea is harsh and brutal to anyone who settles in this green hell. There is heavy mortality from malaria, typhus, dysentery and leprosy.

We landed in a tropical downpour, and were put ashore on a primitive jetty where, nevertheless, the Customs people were tough enough to charge me duty on unexposed camera film, an impost I had never had to suffer anywhere in the civilized world! Port Moresby is an attractive place. Before the war it consisted only of a few tin shacks and barracks; now there are a couple of thousand white inhabitants, modern bungalows, shops and warehouses, even some expensive hotels and, finally, a cinema, which twice a week presents antiquated films. The films are so completely ruined by the damp tropical heat that they cannot be returned to the letting companies in Australia, and when they have been around the island they are burned. Nothing more can be seen through the watery haze that remains on the celluloid!

Port Moresby is enlivened by the charming laughing girls of Papua, dressed in raffia skirts and with flowers in their hair. There is some race discrimination in New Guinea, but it is not very marked: in the shops you can see these attractive brown creatures shopping side by side with faded, tropic-bitten white women. The missionaries have not dressed these gay and carefree girls in cheap cotton dresses and induced in them an artificial sense of shame.

A few miles from Port Moresby lies the large native village, Hanuabada, built in the water on piles. When the tribes from the interior used to raid the coast, the village on stilts was a safe place, as the attackers could seldom swim. The villagers removed the bridges between their huts and the water-line and defended themselves by hurling stones at the thwarted attackers on the shore. Since the Government put an end to these raids, the need for water defences has gone. The missionaries had the idea that it would be better to round up the water-borne heathens on to the mainland where they could more easily keep them under surveillance, and they persuaded many of the pile dwellers to move ashore. The natives naturally built their huts as they had always done—that is, on piles. They carried on life as usual: relieved nature over the side of the veranda, swept the dirt through the cracks in the floor and threw the garbage out of doors. Hitherto the tidal water had coped with the problem of sanitation; but now excrement and rubbish piled up underneath and around the huts where the children and pigs frolicked. It was not long before an epidemic of dysentery broke out and took heavy toll. The natives, naturally, were puzzled when the authorities ordered them to demolish their huts and rebuild them again out in the water on piles. The missionaries had to think up a new way of maintaining a vigilant watch upon their potential converts.

The confusion which arises when white men impinge on native custom and habit was illustrated in another episode when a high-ranking official and his lady were due to visit a certain village. Word was sent ahead to the chief, suggesting that the girls of the village should wear more clothes than usual lest their naked breasts should shock the lady. When the party arrived for the reception, however, the girls were observed to be wearing their usual costume of raffia skirts and flowers in the hair. But as the official's wife stepped ashore all the girls modestly lifted their raffia skirts and held them over their breasts.

I stayed a couple of weeks in Port Moresby; planning my visits to three different districts and securing the permits necessary for the journeys. I bought some stores, including a few bottles of anti-mosquito oil, and generally occupied myself in the thousand preparations for such an expedition. One day I heard a loud, buzzing noise over the hotel, and looking out saw a helicopter performing the oddest manœuvres. It had recently arrived by ship, in sections, consigned to the Australasian Petroleum Company Ltd., who had hired four helicopters from the American Helicopter Company Inc. to use for flights to the inaccessible oil borings of the Fly river delta. One of the machines was being tried out to see how helicopters would behave in a tropical climate. In the hotel later I met a couple of the pilots and the American engineer who was supervising the assembling of the machines. I suggested cheerfully that they should test their helicopter by flying me over the Purari swamps, a few hundred miles west of Port Moresby, where there were said to be some villages isolated from all contact.

The engineer meditated a moment, then said: 'Okay, let's go.'

A few days later he and I set off with food for a couple of days. The helicopter was fitted with a couple of big rubber balloons to enable us to go down on the water for refuelling from our spare cans, although that operation is actually feasible in flight if you have a gift for acrobatics. It was a wonderful feeling to be liberated from the law of gravitation, to rise vertically as if on a flying carpet. From the plastic dome there was a fine view all around. We circled the harbour for a few minutes testing the meters and controls and then set course along the coast towards the north-west. We flew over several outrigger sailing canoes, *lakatois*, and went down mast-high over one of them. The natives aboard the canoe reacted very differently. Some of them waved greetings to us—and others jumped into the water, evidently stricken with fear. We kept inshore where the water was crystal-clear round the coral reefs, and once drifted down for a closer view of a basking shark.

After three hours flying, which included some detours over coastal villages, we reached the edge of the vast mangrove swamps at the mouth of the River Purari, and hovered over them for some time without seeing any signs of life. We followed one of the delta tributaries for a few miles, but soon abandoned the ambition to discover

Ayers Rock: over seven miles round and 1,500 feet high

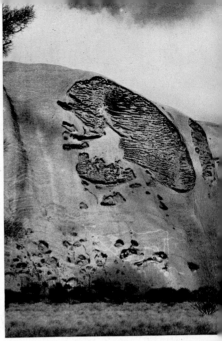

Sandstorms through the centuries have scoured great holes in the granite

A skull-like shape weathered in the face of the rock

Cave-bound for four days, I had ample opportunity to study the ancient rock paintings

The cloudburst which kept us in the cave was the first for seven years

Port Moresby girls in their raffia skirts

hidden villages in this dark-green impenetrable morass of mangrove and mud. If these alleged villages really existed, they must be much deeper in the swamp, and we had not enough petrol to prolong the search. On our way back to the mouth of the river, however, we came upon something which from the filming point of view provided ample compensation for the failure to find the swamp villages: it was a fantastic ghost jungle, a great stretch of dead mangrove trees, which had perished for lack of the sea-water they need. We landed the helicopter and walked among the distorted and barkless trunks which, against the sky, looked as if they had been seized in a convulsion. It was a spectacle which reminded me of Robert Sherwood's 'The Petrified Forest'.

The jungle had a grotesque appearance. The black glistening mud appeared to be infested with prehistoric monsters; miniature dinosaurs, iguanodons, caricatures of dwarf elephants, kangaroos, frogs, giraffes, snakes. But all these freaks of nature were motionless; so, too, were the clusters of what seemed to be the shapes of men. As we looked at these distorted petrified figures we realized that they were the shapes made by the vast tangle of mangrove roots rotting in the swamp and producing these weird patterns from the prehistoric world. The dead swamp was pervaded by a deathly silence; no bird-song, no buzzing of insects; and from the decaying bushes there came a most horrible stench. We had not been long in the swamp when we found that there was some life there after all: swarms of sand-flies attacked us. They were no larger than a grain of sand, but their stings hurt as much as that of a swarm of bees. Because of the choking, humid heat we had taken off our clothes, except for our underpants, and very soon we itched and smarted all over and our skins became red and inflamed.

We caught sight of some mud snails and river prawns, with large lobster-like claws; when we tried to catch them they disappeared into holes in the mud. We also saw a few mud skippers, which looked rather like blennies as they wriggled at an incredible speed across the mud. There were many treacherous places in the swamp, where the rain-water had turned the mud into a glutinous black porridge which sucked at one's feet. Here and there were new green mangrove shoots, which suggested that the swamp was coming to life again. The mangroves had long roots which penetrated deep into the mud and left the bushes standing as if on stilts. It was impossible to break a way through this contorted tangle. The sand-flies gradually became so insufferable that we were forced to retire into the helicopter, where we set the rotary propeller in motion and stood under it to cool ourselves off while we dressed and packed the film camera and filled up again with petrol. The propeller also proved an ideal repellent for the loathsome sand-flies. By now we felt as if we had been badly burned or whipped by nettles. When we circled round, to set course for home, we realized what a unique experience we had had, for it would be impossible to reach this petrified swamp except by helicopter. On our way home an amusing incident occurred. We hovered for a few minutes a few yards above a village on the Orokola coast, where the natives gathered below us, shouting and gesticulating with excitement. They flung some bananas up to us and in return we threw cigarettes down to them, like manna from heaven. When we reached the hangar at Port Moresby towards evening, the pilot and I scratched each other's backs for the last time and declared that Port Moresby's mosquitoes were household pets compared with the venomous sand-flies of the swamp.

7

The Natives Eat the Road: My First Encounter with the Kukukuku Cannibals

At last my preparations in Port Moresby had been completed, and with several hundred pounds of baggage I flew in one of the Government's planes right across the island (which is three times the size of England) to the little town of Lae, on the north coast, where the stifling heat was even more deadly than on the south coast. It was the worst time of the year. The rainy season was over; the sun burned down from a cloudless sky, there was no wind from the ocean, and the earth positively steamed. Fifteen minutes after it had been put on, a clean shirt clung to one's body like a wet rag. One drank perpetually, hoping by the process of sweat and evaporation to keep the temperature of the body at a bearable degree. The town's only hotel had a large bar, a kind of Wild West saloon, with whirring fans, where a mixed bag of men sought relief. There were gold miners, planters, coastal skippers, contractors, works' foremen, civil servants, missionaries. There were local residents and visitors from the coast plantations or from the mountains. The District Commissioner, who was to help me with the planning of my journey into the mountains, was away on a tour of inspection and was not due for another week, so I had ample time and opportunity to share in the relaxations which the bar could offer.

A few days after my arrival, I had a great surprise. A young man standing next to me at the bar downed a glass of cold, frothy beer, belched loudly and said with gusto: 'det var s'gu d-a-j-l-i-g-t!'

Which, in Danish, means, roughly, 'That's better!'

'Did you like it, old boy?' I asked him in Danish.

He whirled around and stared at me. His name, he said, was Henning Pedersen, from Amager; and next to him stood his friend, Albert Quist, from Lyngby. They were both surveyors working for the Government, making roads along the coast up to a gold-mine some distance inland.

'You are the first Dane we have met here,' they said, 'since the *Galatea* was here,' and ordered another round. They were a pair of cheerful, tough boys from Copenhagen, who were ready for anything. A couple of years ago they had been home on leave in Denmark, but in spite of fever, the tropics had got such a hold on them that they returned to New Guinea and renewed their contract with the Government.

I used my enforced idleness to go with them on one of their surveying assignments in the swamp along the coast. The swamp was in many places like a green, slimy wall of moss-covered trees, lianas, bracken and undergrowth, through which we had to hack our way with knives and axes, all the time keeping a look-out for crocodiles, snakes, leeches and other reptiles. No ray of sun or breath of wind penetrated the half-light of this steaming jungle, and as soon as the sun set, the mosquitoes swarmed so thickly that we had immediately to seek shelter under the mosquito nets. In several of the little rivers that wound their way through the mangrove swamp, we met every now and then natives in canoes, either fishing, hunting crocodiles or wild pig.

One day we came across a canoe in which lay a native, semi-conscious with fever and starvation. How long he had been lying there we never found out, as he did not speak the language of the coastal natives, but we suspected him of being a man from the highlands, who had fled from the prison at Lae. We cared for him as well as we could and took him back with us to the hospital at Lae. During the war in the Pacific violent battles were fought on New Guinea's north coast, and the Americans made a road across the swamps south of Lae to transport troops and material. My Danish friends told me: 'The natives have eaten up most of the road.'

'What's that?' I said.

'Yes, practically eaten it up. When the Americans were short of building materials, they took what was nearest at hand. They drove several lorries of cased, preserved meat into the swamps, pressed the cases into the mud in two layers and put planks across them. The natives, however, discovered that there was meat in the roads; so they crept out at night, broke open the cases and devoured, by and by, most of the road. That is why we are plotting a new one. But this time it is going to be stone and concrete—so *bon appétit* to the natives!'

'There are often tribal wars going on up there,' said the District Commissioner of the Morobe District, Mr Horrie Niall, 'and they are still cannibals.' But he gave me a permit to go on and film the Kukukuku tribes in the Menyamya district of the mountains. The permit specified various conditions: The bearer must take weapons in order to protect himself and his party. He must not intervene in differences among the natives when they are not members of his party. No natives on the expedition must

be sent to bargain for food or services with natives outside
the territory under the Commissioner's control. The bearer
must take with him such materials for barter with the
natives as are approved by the District Commissioner.
The bearer must follow the routes indicated by the District
Commissioner or by local patrol officers; and on the way
to and from the territory specified in the permit, the bearer
must not camp in the vicinity of villages or settlements.

'Don't forget,' Mr Niall told me, 'we have only had a
police post up there a few years and we have by no means
got all the tribes under control yet. Large areas have not
been explored or patrolled by white men. The natives get
scared when they see whites and easily get 'arrow-happy'.
We will send a white police officer along with you, and
ten native police; but do not forget, you are travelling
entirely at your own risk. We can fly you and your gear
up in a few days. Make sure you return—and good luck!'

The heavily-laden little Qantas aeroplane wound in and
out between the mountain peaks, some of them festooned
with cotton-wool clouds. The main part of my luggage
was my treasure chest: it consisted of two sacks of *giri giri*,
small white beach shells—and a box of 200 knives and a
few axes. Apart from that I took only the most essential
tinned food, my film equipment and sound recorders. The
pilot, whom I knew by now very well from the bar sessions
in Lae, entertained me by pointing out the spots where
aeroplanes had crashed; and to make things especially
cheerful for me, he made a detour over the wreck of one
which had gone down a month ago. The feats which
pilots attempt and achieve in flying over New Guinea
would send any airport superintendent out of his mind.
Most of the country is a trackless terrain, and in many
places the landings are made actually on the hillside,
because no flat places exist. No insurance company will

touch this inland traffic, and one of the small charter companies had no fewer than four crashes in the fortnight I had already been in New Guinea. After an hour's flight, in which we crossed two very lofty mountain ranges, we caught sight of some white blobs in a green valley far below.

'There is Menyamya,' said the pilot and, circling down, he landed neatly next to a couple of large bamboo huts. It was the Government station of the Menyamya district, the extreme outpost of civilization in this little-known part of New Guinea's mountainous interior. The post had been established a few years ago, after violent battles between the natives, and it was far from safe here even yet. Neither of the two young Australian police officers, Bill Purdy and Jack Mater, who lived here, ventured beyond the station without an armed escort. The valley of Menyamya lay over four thousand feet up; the only communication with the outer world was by plane and radio. The purpose of the outpost was to serve as a base for surveying and pacifying the district, and from it to contact the natives and endeavour to put down their tribal warfare and cannibal orgies. The Kukukuku tribes had always spread terror among the people living around them.

These terrible little mountain people are supposed to have been given their name by the Papuans on the south coast whom they have so often raided. It is a rude and derisive nickname based on the supposedly homosexual propensities of these ferocious little cannibals. They never call themselves the Kukukukus, but employ different names for each tribal sub-group according to the locality they inhabit, such as Menyer, Huatuaer, Boungaer, Mankier, Nautier, Kwondanyer and Jagentsaer. Between them they occupy a territory about the size of Denmark; each group lives isolated from the others, and they speak different dialects. When they call on each other it is usually to kill. How many Kukukukus there are is not exactly known; the estimate is somewhere between 50,000 and 100,000. The measure of their power to terrorize neighbouring tribes is shown by the fact that a whole coastal village would flee in terror if only four or five Kukukukus came in sight. As it happened I saw two of these notorious cannibals the moment I jumped out of the plane to greet the two patrol officers, Bill Purdy and Jack Mater. The Kukukukus stood together in a little group, thick-set and strongly built, each wearing a tuft of grass in front, a small bone through the nose, and with bows and clubs in their hands. There were no women among them.

'These live quite close by and are peaceful enough now,' Jack Mater told me. 'They turn up every time a plane arrives. First time they saw one they thought it was a great bird, mother of the white men who climbed out of its belly. They went over to the plane and put some sweet potatoes under its nose so that it could eat.'

Mr Niall, in Lae, had warned Menyamya by the radio of my visit and of its objects, which were to film the life of the natives and make sound recordings for the Australian Broadcasting Corporation. It turned out that Jack Mater was about to start a reconnaissance patrol into the mountains, to villages which had not previously been visited, and so was able to take me under his wing. Three days later we set off, before sunrise, a caravan of fifty-four in all: forty-two carriers rounded up from adjacent villages, eight native armed police, two interpreters, Jack and myself. The policemen were fine upstanding fellows from the coast who did not speak the language of the Kukukukus.

The caravan wound like a gigantic snake along the rudimentary tracks higher and higher up the grassy

gle and Swamp: we kept a look-out for crocodiles and leeches

Leaving for the swamp

The black glutinous mud seemed alive with fantastic creatures fossilized
in their embryonic stage

mountain slopes. The police, some ahead and some in the rear, kept one eye on the carriers in case any of them should think of bolting with his load. Every now and then the carriers would start a song which in the morning stillness echoed down into the valley which was now disappearing from view below. The weather in these highlands was much better than along the coast: like a warm summer day in Europe. Most of the time we kept to the tracks; but at some points we made short cuts through the tall, stiff grass, called *kunai*, which covered the slopes and in places grows three or four feet high. This tough tenacious grass is kept down because the natives set fire to it whenever they go through it, sometimes to catch the small animals which hide in it, sometimes to signal to members of their tribe in distant villages and, quite often, simply to satisfy their natural pyromaniac desire to see flames and smoke devour the long slopes. In the weeks to come I was to see many of these grass fires, which sent vast clouds into the sky and left big, black patches on the green slopes. The smoke sometimes destroyed the visibility so completely as to prevent flying over large areas of New Guinea.

Only on the hill-tops and in the gorges was any vegetation to be found, except the *kunai* grass. In these there were pandanus palms, fern trees, conifers and bamboo; and an abundance of creeping plants, wild sugar-cane, bracken and mosses; there were very few flowers. I learned later that practically all the plants in the jungle are used by the natives for some purpose or other; either for food or for building their huts, or for weapons, tools and magic rituals. I noticed that in some places we made a wide detour round a certain kind of tree. This was a 'spirit tree', I was told, where the dead forefathers' spirits sit on the branches and do not like their privacy to be disturbed.

After marching about nine or ten miles we came to the

village of Kwondanya, perched high on a rising slope. The villagers had been watching our approach for some time and now they started to call down to us as we drew nearer. Jack Mater had been there a few times previously, and said it was unlikely that they would take to their heels as so often happened when a reconnaissance patrol arrived at a village. When we got into the village the women had all disappeared; but the men came to meet us with bamboo sticks filled with drinking water, a recognized gesture of welcome. They drank some of it themselves first before handing it to us, to show that it was safe to drink, an action which I found most reassuring, because they looked anything but peaceful. Not for a moment did they let go of their bows and arrows and stone clubs.

There were two types of hut. One was circular with a grass roof which went right down to the ground and concealed the entrance to the hut. The other type was either round or square, but with much higher walls, and the floor, made of split bamboo sticks, was raised a foot or two above the ground. The roof of this type was made of dried pandanus leaves which hardened to the toughness of corrugated iron. When a cottage was left empty, the entrance was often barricaded with tree trunks and branches heaped up in front of it, and the same practice was followed when the residents retired for the night. Every family appeared to have three or four huts each surrounded by fences made of pointed bamboo sticks. The entrances were so low that one had to bend down to crawl through them. The Kukukukus took no chances. Later on I saw settlements defended, not only by bamboo stockades, but also by a deep moat outside the stockade.

Some of our carriers came from Kwondanya, and were pleased when they heard we were going on to another village, Kiwogwonga, higher up. It had only once before been visited by a patrol which was sent there to stop an outbreak of fighting. The carriers obviously assumed we were going to make an attack on this village, for before leaving they helped themselves to an extra supply of arrows. The Kiwogwonga people were notorious for their bloodthirsty behaviour and had earlier on been in trouble with the Kwondanya. It was late in the afternoon when we reached Kiwogwonga, after a ten hours march uphill to about seven thousand feet, and I was exhausted. Jack had all along been taking bearings to mark upon his chart, which was based solely on air photographs. The village of scattered huts lay on a small plateau, thickly covered with trees and shrub. As our caravan drew near the village there was not a soul to be seen.

'They have hidden in the thicket,' said Jack. 'No doubt their arrows are pointing straight at us this very minute, but I doubt if they will dare to loose off; we are too many for them.'

The carriers were ordered to sit down on the ground, the soldiers were told to have their rifles at the ready, but not to aim. A few tense minutes passed during which I took care to get out of the front line of fire. On Jack's order a tarpaulin was spread out on the ground within view of the thicket, and a pile of sea-shells and knives was put on it. Jack told the interpreter to shout into the thicket to tell them that we were friends and that we had presents for the village. There was no reply. He repeated the assurance a few times, but still without evoking a response of any kind. The carrier began to get nervous and to shuffle around. The tarpaulin was moved nearer to the thicket. Jack and I withdrew a little, together with the policemen. We sat down and lit cigarettes to appear as nonchalant as possible.

'They must have bad consciences, since they do not

come out,' said Jack. 'They must have done something lately which they think they are going to be punished for —an eating orgy perhaps, or else they have murdered some of the neighbours. We shall have to settle down here a bit and try to find out what it is.'

Suddenly a couple of warriors appeared by the tarpaulin, so swiftly that we hardly saw where they came from. The interpreter told them that we wanted to buy sweet potatoes from them, and upon that the men vanished again into the thicket. Ten minutes later all the inhabitants of the village started to come out: first the men, then the women and children. Within an hour the strained atmosphere had completely disappeared. The Kiwogwonga people built a large hut for us of bamboo and pandanus leaves just outside the village. We sent most of the carriers back having paid each of them a handful of beach-shells. They did not, in any case, wish to go farther into enemy country and we could get fresh carriers from Kiwogwonga. The policemen raised a flagpole outside the hut and very soon the Australian Government flag bearing the Southern Cross was waving in the afternoon sun.

8

We Catch a Murderer: Close-up of Cannibals: The Children Stone the Prisoners to Death: Chant of Death

WE decided to stay in the village of Kiwogwonga for a few days to 'show the flag', for we had a feeling that something suspicious was going on among the people, and we noted their apprehensive looks, whispered conversations and attitude of general reserve. Jack was determined to find out what was afoot. I noticed that there were hardly any old men in the village. 'No,' said Jack, 'If you see an old man here you may be sure that he is either a redoubtable warrior or a notable coward; otherwise he wouldn't be alive——!' 'It is difficult to stop them killing each other,' he went on. 'Human lives mean nothing to them. I'll tell you what happened a few months ago when I came to a village to buy sweet potatoes for my carriers. One of the men of the village came and offered me some, but at the same moment another man pushed himself forward, so as to offer *his* potatoes. The first one, with his free hand, pulled a club out of his grass belt and bashed the other one on the head and half-killed him. After that, he did not even give a glance at the beaten competitor, but kept on offering me his potatoes! Killing for them is merely a sport. The young men are not really considered worth while until they have killed somebody. There is only one thing that can make them stop, and that is superior force and the fear of consequences. Every time we hear of a murder, it is imperative that we catch the murderer and punish him, and if we hear of an attack on a village, we must be off to punish the aggressors, generally by burning down their huts. It is a hard policy, but the only effective one.'

I did not take many films for the first few days. The women, especially, were terrified when the camera was pointed at them; but on the contrary they were not in the least afraid of the tape recorder, and they were enthralled when they heard themselves speak or shout on the playback. Through the interpreter, we gradually discovered what the inhabitants were trying to hide from us. One of the young men of the village had, a few weeks back, committed a murder in a small village a few miles away. There had been a murder 'owing' in that village and this young man, who had not been on a raid before, had stolen off on his own to one of the rival village plantations, where he had cloven the head of a woman who was working peacefully, and returned home to receive the plaudits of the whole village.

As soon as he had seen our caravan drawing near, he had run away, and was in hiding somewhere. Partly by the gleanings of the interpreters and partly by bribery we found out in a few days that the murderer was concealed in a neighbouring ravine where the youths of the village visited him by day. At night he came back to his two young wives to a hut outside the village. We planned a raid. I was wakened at three o'clock in the morning by Jack shaking my camp bed. Outside it was cold, and a damp mist enveloped everything. Police Sergeant Maga, who knew of the plan, was ready with four police and off we crept through the village. Although we were going as quietly as possible we awoke one of the warriors who, seeing the soldiers, concluded we were out to kill him. We promised him a knife if he would show us the place where the murderer was hiding, and at this invitation he looked greatly relieved.

For safety's sake we placed him between two of the policemen and started off in single file in the direction he indicated. The path, which was slippery from rain and mist, wound down a steep, rocky mountain slope on which we often had to catch hold of grass and bushes, so as not to tumble down in the dark. We had only brought a couple of torches with us. After an hour's difficult climbing and slithering down the slope it began to get light, and we could catch a glimpse of some fenced-in fields and a cluster of huts further down. These huts are not meant for permanent residence, but as a shelter against the rain. Suddenly Sergeant Maga gave a suppressed cry of pain and bent sharply down. Jack and I ran forward, thinking for a moment that he had been hit by an arrow; but he whispered, 'Stop Master, booby-traps,' and pulled a long, sharp bamboo spike out of his naked foot. We examined the path more carefully, and saw that in several places these bamboo spikes had been put into the ground and camouflaged with leaves and grass. The murderer had, evidently, taken his precautions against surprise. Only Jack and I wore boots, so we crept on ahead and, as quietly as possible, forced the spikes into the ground or broke them off short. When we at last reached the huts, we saw smoke coming from one of them and our guide confirmed that this was where the murderer was hiding. We carefully surrounded the hut.

'We won't use the entrance,' Jack whispered, 'perhaps he has set a trap for us there, and he mustn't have a chance to get away from us. I'll jump through the roof

with these,' he added, producing a couple of handcuffs.
'You can follow if you feel like it.' He took off in a long
leap and disappeared, handcuffs, torch and legs, down
through the roof of the hut. Without stopping to think I
followed him by the same route. For a few seconds all
was pandemonium. I landed lightly, but in pitch dark.
Arms and legs were threshing about and I heard some
unearthly sounds. At last Jack got his torch working, and
by its light I saw the terrified eyes of a young native
fumbling around for his weapons. Jack bore down on
him, and in a few seconds had the handcuffs on the man,
who was so blinded and confused by the light as to put
up little resistance. There were two screaming women in
the little hut who crawled over us to the door where they
ran right into the arms of the waiting police. We let them
go at once, and they fled wailing and lamenting. The whole
thing took only a few seconds. I gave a sigh of relief when
it was all over, and discovered that I had collected a couple
of nasty burns on one knee from a little fire burning on the
floor of the hut. We all sat down and had a smoke, including
the murderer, to calm our nerves, and to watch the dawn
over the mountains to the east; then we started for home.

It was full daylight when we got back to Kiwogwonga.
The murderer, who had admitted his guilt at once, was
put into the police hut. The rest of the day was marked
by great agitation in the village. A dozen of the men
gathered outside the 'prison', shouting and gesticulating
to have the prisoner set free. When they began to get
really aggressive, Jack ordered all the police to line up,
and the muscular Sergeant Maga, with a face of iron and
a voice like a roaring lion, gave them a quarter of an
hour's rifle exercise. The natives interpreted this drill as
the prelude to an execution and soon abandoned their
threatening attitude.

Late in the afternoon there was a moving occurrence. An old woman, completely covered in mud and clay, as a sign of sorrow, came to our hut leading a large pig. She was the mother of the prisoner and wanted to buy him back in exchange for the pig. She firmly believed that we were going to kill him and eat him, even though, through the interpreter, we told her that he would return to her in due course. This she evidently could not believe and she so worked upon the villagers that we had to chase her away. That night we slept with our rifles in our camp beds, and the policemen stood watches. But all was peaceful. Early in the morning, before the village was awake, the prisoner, under guard, was sent off down to the post at Menyamya. From here he was flown across to Lae, where he paid the penalty for his crime by cutting grass for six months. The worst part of his punishment was doubtless the flight in the aeroplane, an ordeal which terrifies these natives to such an extent that they lose all control of their physical functions. When a prisoner returns to his people after serving his sentence he never tells his relatives what he has experienced; he believes he has been in a hell which does not bear description.

The day after the despatch of the prisoner, we said good-bye to Kiwogwonga, hired some new carriers and continued the trek east across hills and valleys, rivers and ravines to a group of small villages which had not previously been visited by any patrol or any white man. We were going to move the white man's milestone a little distance farther. From afar we could see the villages, a medley of gardens and huts strategically disposed in the green, hilly landscape so that the villagers could see any would-be attackers a long way off. It was near one of these villages that the murderer from Kiwogwonga, a few weeks ago, had killed the woman in the plantation. We hoped the fact that we could tell the villagers that we had punished the murderer would ensure us a friendly reception.

We were right. When, an hour before sunset, we reached the first of the little settlements, we found that almost all the inhabitants had fled into the jungle; but some of the men remained within ear-shot, their bows and arrows at the ready. When our interpreters called to them not to be afraid, that we only wanted to buy sweet potatoes, they all came towards us at once; and when we told them that we had caught the man from Kiwogwonga who had killed one of their women, they were elated, and asked us if we would help them to kill all the Kiwogwongas! After all, they said, we claimed to be their friends! Those of the Kiwogwonga carriers who were still with us were visibly relieved when they understood from the interpreter that we had declined this pressing offer of alliance. But as soon as they had been paid their wages of a handful of sea-shells, they went off in a hurry in spite of the fact that it was already getting dark and that they would have to sleep *en route*. The villagers quickly ran up a couple of huts for us before it became quite dark. In the following four weeks we made our base here while I made the first documentary film ever produced of the Kukukukus' daily life.

The Kukukukus lived a very primitive life, dominated in every way by the laws of the jungle. They went in constant fear of attack and themselves lost no opportunity of aggression. The women plodded all day long with their digging-sticks in the fields or endlessly sought and carried fuel, while the men roamed about hunting, burning the grass slopes to make new clearings, building huts or making weapons; but always, whatever they were doing, alert for battle. As none of the land is flat, their fields are all situated on slopes. They take little trouble to prepare the

soil, and after the grass has been burned off, the women
get to work digging with their sticks. The men fell trees,
either with stone axes or by keeping fires going against
the trunk until it burns through and collapses. They often
put fences around the fields to keep the wild pig away.
They grow mainly *kau kau*, sweet potatoes, and these
tubers taste excellent when roasted in ashes. I lived on
them all the time I was with the Kukukukus, and when I
returned to civilization found that I had completely lost
my taste for ordinary potatoes which seem to have a less
decided flavour.

Apart from *kau kau* they grow a few other root plants
such as taro, and in between the sweet potatoes they
generally grow sugar-cane. They also plant various banana
trees, but these are flavourless cooked, and cannot be
eaten raw. Most of their other vegetables, among them
long beans, grow wild in the jungle, where the women
pick them. Green bamboo shoots, which look like green
asparagus, they regard as a delicacy. There are always
plenty of nuts and mushrooms in the jungle. If the fields
are far from the village, there is usually a little hut built
there, sometimes only a roofed-in shed, where they can
seek shelter from the rain or have a nap when they are
working long hours. During the day-time there was always
much going and coming between the village and the fields.
The women would come trudging along bearing on their
backs nets filled with *kau kau* and other produce. On top
of the load there might be a baby rolled in a shawl, and
balanced on their shoulders firewood or bamboo sticks full
of water. The babies were often hung up in their nets
outside the hut while the women worked nearby.

The Kukukukus have not yet learned to make clay
utensils, so they cook their food in large hollowed-out
bamboo sticks, which are put directly on to the fire. It is

an excellent method, and I have often eaten very good wild pig cooked in this way. Another way of cooking is to roll the food in pieces of bark and put them on the embers. Bigger meals are cooked by digging a hole in the ground and putting hot stones and embers in the bottom of it. The food is then wrapped in leaves, put on top of the stones and covered up with a thin layer of soil, to keep the heat in.

Drinking water is brought from the mountain streams in hollow bamboo sticks. Altogether the bamboo seems to be the plant most used by the Kukukukus. Apart from using it for cooking utensils and water containers, they also make knives, pipes, flutes, torches and arrows from bamboo. A bamboo knife is so sharp that a wild pig's carcass can be cut up with it as easily as with a sharp steel butcher's knife. They also shave their heads with a bamboo knife. When a bamboo knife becomes blunt, they just tear off a couple of fibres with their teeth, and then have a completely new, sharp edge. The bamboo pipes are very simply operated. They stuff the tobacco into one end of a short hollow bamboo containing a filter of nutshells, and suck the smoke out of the other end. The pipes, as a rule, pass round the group from one to the other, although I have only seen a few Kukukukus smoke. They grow the tobacco in the fields and dry the leaves over a slow fire in the huts. They seem to be chewing betel practically all the time, and their mouths are always an ominous blood-red colour from this habit. Their bow-strings, too, are made of bamboo, by splitting the bark into narrow widths which are surprisingly strong. If a bow-string breaks, they can make and fit a new one in a few minutes.

When the Kukukukus go out at night, which is rare, because they are afraid of the spirits, they carry long bamboos as torches. The bamboo, which may be two or

three yards long, is split at one end, and into the gash
there are put burning pieces of bark. The flutes are usually
'pan flutes', with only two or three holes. On a special
occasion, though, I saw a strange flute of exceptional size
made from a four- or five-yard-long bamboo, with holes
bored into it at several points. The flute was standing
outside a hut, where the wind caught it and gave out a
melodious sound which rose and fell with the strength of
the wind. This was the only specimen I saw and I believe
it was the special contrivance of the inhabitant of the hut.
Or, perhaps, it had been picked up by barter on the coast.

The ubiquitous bamboo also provides the means of
kindling fire. You take a dry stick, split one end and put a
small stone into the crack to keep it open. Then you put
a bit of dried moss, grass or crushed leaves into the crack,
lay the stick on the ground with its cracked end resting
on some more kindling, and hold it down with your foot.
You then take a ribbon or fibre of bamboo and 'saw' it to
and fro through the crack. Within a few seconds the dried
moss in the crack is alight. You apply it to a heap of dry
grass—and there is your fire! I say 'you', but I did not
manage the trick myself. I tried several times but was only
able to produce a mild smouldering. The bamboo, then,
is the basic material of economy among the Kukukukus;
without it they would have difficulty in surviving.

Like all natives the Kukukukus always enjoy meat; even
the merest fragment, together with sweet potatoes, makes
an acceptable meal for them. But it was always a problem
for them to procure enough, and for days on end they would
have to make do with vegetables. Many of them did,
indeed, keep kanaka pigs; but these represented such
economic riches that they were reserved for special
occasions and ceremonies. In the jungle wild pig were
scanty and difficult to kill. When the Kukukukus went

hunting they were sometimes lucky enough to bag a rock
kangaroo or a *cassowary*, a bird like an ostrich, and then
they would have meat for several days. Or they might kill
a possum, which very much resembles a squirrel, with a
thick spiral tail. Other jungle delicacies were rats, field-
mice, snakes, lizards and big, white caterpillars from the
roots of rotting trees. I myself tried a couple of roast
caterpillars; like the ones I ate in the Australian desert,
they reminded me of crisp pork-crackling.

There were also to be had cockatoos and wood-pigeons
which they shot with arrows from well-camouflaged hide-
outs among the trees. Birds of paradise they shot more for
the feathers than the meat. Even with these small targets
their marksmanship was remarkable, and up to twenty
yards, or even eighty, they never missed. They used traps,
too, for hunting. The commonest was a heavy block of wood
poised on some sticks among which the bait was planted.
When an animal tried to get the bait it would dislodge
a stick and bring down the block on its back. They also
constructed little pit-falls, with sharp bamboo spikes at
the bottom, and camouflaged with branches and leaves.
These traps were always marked by a couple of sticks
arranged in a special way to warn passers-by. If a man
found an animal in someone else's trap, he would always
bring the catch to the owner of the trap. If he were to
steal the animal for himself, and the theft were discovered,
he would be forced to pay compensation, or be run out of
the community.

I saw no fishing, but I was told that they sometimes
fished down in the Tauri river, below the Menyamya valley.
Their method was to build a small dam and thus lower
the water below so that they could see the fish, which they
would then shoot with their arrows. I never saw them bathe
or swim in their rivers; if the water was too deep to wade

through, they cut down a tree so that it fell on the opposite side of the river. When the men were not hunting, building huts or making clearings they sat in little clusters outside their huts and worked on their weapons, of which they took great care. They always had a good supply of arrows, of different types, for various purposes. The arrow shafts were made of wild sugar-cane or of bamboo shoots; the arrow-heads were cut from hard palm wood and bound on with a kind of raffia. The bows were made of palm branches, cut to shape with a flint or a wild pig's tooth. It might take them no more than a month to cut and grind the head of a stone club. These had different shapes; some resembled a thick, flat plate with a hole in the middle for the shaft; others were star-shaped. Their wooden clubs were fashioned from palm wood and looked like a large knotty pineapple. Their stone axes were made simply by fastening a sharpened stone to a strong V-shaped stick. Their remaining standard weapon was a large, oval wooden shield. Even if they had not been in contact with Europeans some of the men had often possessed themselves of long steel knives got by barter from neighbouring tribes, or else captured from them.

Whenever the men left the huts, either to go hunting or to go to the fields, they always took their weapons with them. They were always ready either for defence or attack. They maintained a constant distrust of their neighbours; but towards us, who were complete strangers, their attitude was different. I gave them various presents in exchange for the specimens I gathered for the National Museum of Denmark; I joked with them, showed them photographs of other natives and let them listen to the tape recorder. They had an attractive, spontaneous sense of humour, and there was something very touching in the pleasure they evidently felt at meeting strangers who manifestly intended them no mischief. The children would come to clutch my arm if they wanted to show me something. The boys roared with laughter at my unskilful efforts to compete with them with bow and arrow.

It was difficult to imagine that these people were cannibals; but one day I was given a sudden revelation of their blood-lust. I had bought one of their tame pigs, and asked the headman of the village, a young warrior by the name of Momakowa, to kill it for me. He was normally a calm, peaceable fellow, not without a certain natural dignity; but when he set about killing the pig with his club, the joy of slaughter shone in his eyes and he battered the club again and again upon the head of the beast, although it had been killed by the first blow. He kept on till the blood spurted out; the children and women, who had gathered round him, screamed with delight. That incident enabled me to appreciate the reports of the reconnaissance patrols, and to believe what Jack had told me of the barbarous habits of the Kukukukus.

When a party of warriors takes an enemy prisoner, either in combat or by abduction, they tie the captive to a thin tree-trunk and bring him horizontally back to the village. So that the prisoner shall not escape, they then break his legs with a blow of the club, bind him to a tree, and adorn him with shells and feathers in preparation for the forthcoming orgy. Fresh vegetables are brought in from the fields and a big hole is dug in the ground for an oven. As a rule, the children are allowed to 'play' with the 'prisoner'; that is to say, to use him as a target, and finally stone him to death. This process is designed to harden the children and teach them to kill with rapture. When the prisoner has been killed, his arms and legs are cut off with a bamboo knife. The meat is then cut up into small pieces, wrapped in bark, and cooked, together with

A world inhabited by fabulous monsters—dwarf elephants. . . .

and dinosaurs—the crazy zoology of a nightmare

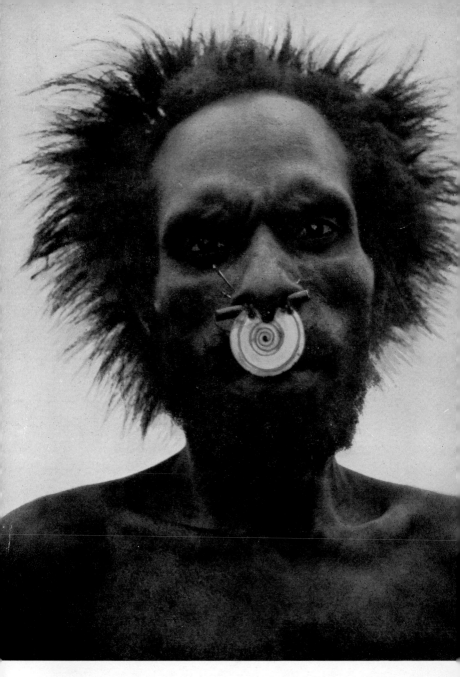

We found a canoe in which lay the above native semi-conscious with malaria

the vegetables, in the oven in the ground. Men, women and children all take part in the ensuing orgy, usually to the accompaniment of dances and jubilant songs. Only enemies are eaten. If the victim is a young strong warrior, the muscular parts of his body are given to the village boys so that they can absorb the dead man's power and valour. Although cannibalism has a certain magic significance, it derives mainly from a shortage of meat, a deficiency of proteins. Meat is a rare luxury for the Kukukukus, and I have often seen them, after burning grass off a hillside, devour with relish the charred corpses of rats, mice, lizards and other vermin.

Jack told me that, six months ago, two men had been eaten in a village, Jagentsaga, not far away; and that a month ago he had, by chance, found the hand of a man who had been eaten shortly beforehand. The rest of him had been hidden in the jungle. 'They know,' he said, 'that we will punish them for cannibalism, so they do everything to conceal it now. But it still occurs and probably will do so for a long time.'

It was a strange feeling to live among these friendly, uninhibited natives and realize that they were cannibals. With the help of the interpreter, and through the agency of my camera and sound recorder, I managed to get closer and closer to their daily lives. The recording which impressed me most was the 'killing' chant made by an instrument called the *tumbu-lun*, a small, flat elongated pipe tied with bark fibre to a long stick. When the men hold their initiation ceremonies at holy places in the jungle, they swing these *tumbu-luns* over their heads during the night so that their sound will keep evil spirits away from the place. The sound is well suited for that purpose; it is a macabre drone somewhat resembling the sound of huge wings. Only fully initiated men may use, or even see, the *tumbu-lun;* no woman must ever hear its sound. If that should happen they believe she would become possessed by the spirit of the *tumbu-lun* and would be made away with. Unfortunately I had no opportunity to witness an initiation ceremony, but I did manage to persuade some of the men in the village to go into the jungle with me one night and swing the *tumbu-lun* there so I could make a recording of its eerie music. The sound it made, of droning, whirring wings, was unnerving, and I could well imagine what hallucinations of hovering spirits the noise would produce in these primitive people.

I learned that one must be careful when dealing with spirits. The following day, when preparing to record a conversation between an old man and an old woman, I inadvertently wound a few feet of the previous recording backwards, and by mistake started the playback instead of the recording. There it came, out of the loudspeaker, the ominous music of the *tumbu-lun*. The old woman stiffened at once, as if struck by lightning, a terrified expression on her face. I switched off at once. For a second or two she sat absolutely without moving; then bolted, screaming with fear. The interpreter and some of the others managed to catch her, but it took the interpreter more than half an hour to convince her that, in the circumstances, she would not be possessed by an evil spirit and that she was not going to die. To calm her further, I gave her a little piece of cloth as a charm.

When I told Jack of the episode, he was very worried about the old woman.

'Her solid belief in the evil spirits *might* have killed her,' he said.

I promised myself to handle the potent spirits with more care in the future.

9

The Magic Rituals of the Kukukukus: Smoking the Corpses: The Skeletons on the Mountain Top

THE Kukukukus use many of the plants and bushes of the jungle for ritual purposes as well as for food, for they believe that certain plants possess magic power. Several of these rituals seemed unintelligible to white men, and it was very difficult to find out what lay behind these ceremonies. When the men, for instance, had to lift a heavy tree-trunk, they first took the branch of a certain bush and swung it a few times over the tree-trunk. Then, they explained, it became lighter to lift. When, after carrying the trunk a little way, they got tired, they repeated the performance, and of course regained their breath in the process. Before the men went on the war-path or out hunting, they generally took with them branches from another kind of bush, and swung these in front of their eyes—to sharpen their sight, they said, and so improve their marksmanship. Another method of ensuring a better aim was to rub the end of the bow with a certain leaf. After such precautions as these they felt safer and more self-confident, and that probably is the psychological explanation of why the medicine-men have thought up these rituals. When a man went hunting he would sometimes leave sticks across the path behind him so that malignant spirits should not follow him and scare the animals away. The mothers crumble large, soft, fern leaves in their hands and rub their babies' bodies with them to make the children grow big and strong. The same leaves are put into the carrier net in which the baby lies, coiled up, as if still in the mother's womb. The women also plant protective herbs between the vegetables in their fields, to ensure a good crop.

One of the oddest of Kukukuku superstitions is the habit of the men, when on the war-path, of chewing a certain plant before going to sleep. Its effect, they claim, is to enable them to hold their water until morning: that is to say, they do not have to go outside the hut and risk being attacked by a watching foe. So one can well appreciate why this plant is essential in a warrior's outfit.

Jack told me how he had witnessed a medicine-man expelling an evil spirit from a sick boy who worked at the post. When the boy became ill, his father and mother came from their village to see him, and brought the medicine-man with them. All three sat down beside the boy and chewed leaves and bark which the medicine-man produced. Then they spat it out over the boy, and the two men started to whip the boy with branches dipped in water, while the mother blew on him, shook him and pulled his hair violently: all to drive out the evil spirit. Suddenly the medicine-man picked up some of the leaves and excitedly tore them to pieces in his hand. He passed the fragments on to the father who, clutching them in his hands, ran down to the river and threw them into the running water. It was the evil spirit which had been coaxed out of the boy and thrown away. The boy recovered ten days later, whatever the reason may have been!

Each day I used to go with one of the interpreters and a couple of police to film the natives at their various activities. I should have preferred to be without the escort as their presence often inhibited natives; but it was a definite order from the District Commissioner in Lae that I was not to go about alone. However, I was never for a moment conscious of any hostile feelings among these charming cannibals. They allowed me to film all aspects of their ceremonial life, even the smoking of their dead. This gruesome practice of preserving the dead, though horrible to witness, has rather pathetic motives.

One day I asked the headman of the village, Moma-kowa, what had happened to the woman whom the Kiwogwonga man had killed. He answered that she still lived in her hut over there, pointing to a little settlement of seven or eight huts on a hillside half a mile away.

'*Lives* there?' I asked, rather puzzled.

'Yes, they are smoking her,' the interpreter translated Momakowa's answer.

The following day I went, with my usual escort, over to the dead woman's settlement. There was no doubt which hut she was in, for outside it sat a group of relatives smeared in mud and clay as a sign of mourning, while from the chimney came a steady cloud of smoke. I sat down and spoke to them for a while and found out that they were the dead woman's husband, her daughters and sisters. They did not mind my going inside, and so down I got and crawled through the orifice. At first I could see nothing, because of the smoke, and what I was most aware of was the repulsive sickly-sweet smell of decay. As my eyes grew used to the darkness, I caught a glimpse of a small fire under a bamboo platform against one side of the wall. On this was placed the corpse of the woman sitting upright, her arms, legs and head tied firmly to bamboo sticks. The stench was unbearable, so I remained inside only a few minutes. As I was anxious to film the corpse, I asked her relations if they would mind carrying it outside the hut. Two of the daughters at once crawled inside the hut and presently emerged carrying the body, which they gently laid down on top of some pieces of bark which the Kukukukus use as capes. They treated their dead mother as if she were still alive. They propped her up comfortably and supported her head, all the time chasing the flies away from her face. I was told that the husband, as well as the daughters, slept by the corpse during the night.

The two daughters' concern for the dead body was very moving, but for all that the sight of the corpse was revolting. The skin had been scorched almost black and had shrunk, like parchment, into folds and wrinkles. Considering that it was now six weeks since the woman had been killed, the corpse was well preserved. It was easy to see where the club had hit her. The skull had been completely split, but her relatives had sewn the skin together again, and in their care for her well-being they had even stuffed food into her mouth. None of them seemed to be in the least aware of the dreadful stench which, even in the open, was overpowering many yards away. The daughters now carried the corpse back into the hut again while I sat talking with the others for an hour or more. I noticed that some of them had peculiar scratches and bloody scars on their faces—the self-inflicted marks of mourning. With the help of the interpreter I succeeded in getting a fairly clear picture of the Kukukukus' death ceremonies.

The Kukukukus believe that when a person dies his spirit hovers near the corpse for enough time to make sure that the funeral rites are properly carried out. They similarly believe that when a person is asleep the spirit leaves the body and wanders about in the dark. A Kukukuku never wakens a sleeping friend too suddenly, for his spirit

86

must have time to return to the body. The near relatives of the dead often give way to wildly hysterical expressions of grief. They cover themselves in mud, throw themselves on the ground beside the corpse, eat soil, tear their hair and beat themselves with sharp flints until the blood streams from them. They maintain these lamentations for four or five days and nights. The women are more indefatigable mourners than the men; and they also inflict more wounds upon themselves than the men do. You can meet old Kukukuku women with their foreheads a mass of scars from the many 'wakes' they have attended. These violent expressions of sorrow are doubtless designed, in some degree, to placate the hovering spirit and ensure that it shall not molest the bereaved.

Not all corpses are smoked; those of children, for example, are, after a few days, chucked into the jungle or down a ravine. But most adults are smoked. The process starts, as a rule, five or six days after death. A small platform is built, the corpse is tied on to it, and for the first week or so the fire is kept going under the platform day and night. Subsequently the fire is lit every third or fourth day. The heat from the fire causes the skin of the corpse to rise in little blisters, and the relatives rub the skin of the corpse with softened bark and take care that nothing from the corpse drips on to the soil, for in that case, the spirit of the dead would be swallowed up and lost in the earth.

The heat gradually makes the corpse swell, and to prevent it from bursting they thrust hollow bamboo sticks into it to release all the fluids, and these, again, they collect on bits of bark so that nothing from the body shall touch the soil. After six to ten weeks the smoking is finished, and by then the corpse has shrunk to a leathery mummy weighing only half of its original weight.

'What happens to the corpses at the end of the smoking?' I asked.

'They are put up there,' answered one of the relatives, pointing to a mountain top five or six miles away.

Before I left the settlement, I asked the women if they would let me hear how they wailed when they were mourning, as I wanted a recording of it. They had no objection, and immediately began their cries. Even though it was an imitation performance they gradually got carried away by their simulated grief and I could hear their lamentations long after I had left the place.

A few days later, while Jack was taking a census in the village, I climbed, with a couple of the policemen, to the cemetery on top of the mountain. It took us five hours to climb, and the final scramble to the platform which acted as a cemetery was the worst experience I had in New Guinea. By a slow progress of finger-holds and toe-holds I crept, an inch at a time, up and across a horrible stretch of rock. Suddenly one foot slipped, and in a moment my whole weight was on my fingers, which themselves had a very sketchy hold. Ten yards below was an abyss of ragged rocks. I felt everything stiffen inside me, and as the last strength left my fingers, I wondered, for a few frightening seconds, how soon it would be before I dropped off.

Just as I was giving up hope, I felt support under one foot, and a calm voice said:

'Okay, Master.'

I turned my head a little, and saw below me an alert brown face. One of the policemen, Angu, who had been climbing behind me had immediately grasped the situation when he heard the rock break off under my foot, and quickly drawing his bayonet had stuck it into a crack in the rock and stepped up on to it. By stretching up on this precarious perch, and clinging to the rock side, he could

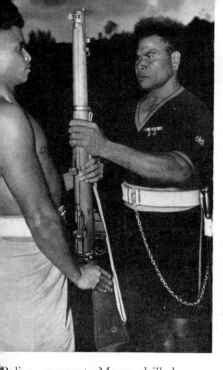

Police sergeant Maga drilled
them for fifteen minutes

The Kukukuku never leave their
village unarmed

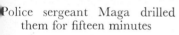

The police-escort carry me across a mountain stream

A Kukukuku in full war paint

The Kukukuku greeting

Crossing the river with firewood

The mother's cape is made from beaten bark

The young murderer was brought back to the camp in handcuffs

just manage to put his fist under my foot, giving me enough support to renew my grip and pull myself up by my arms.

I shall never forget the sight that greeted me as I heaved myself finally over the edge of the cliff and came face to face with a skull only a yard away from me. Angu threw me up a stone, tied to a thin rope, and with this I hauled him up too, while the other soldier stood guard below. I was not too sure that the Kukukukus would approve of my visiting their burial ground. On the platform, which was narrow and protected by overhanging rocks, was a long bench of tree-trunks. On it were a couple of mummies, propped in an upright position; and apart from them ten or twelve more-or-less collapsed skeletons lay about the bench. The mummies, which smelled horribly, were full of ants, caterpillars and other vermin, and the whole platform was thick with bird droppings. How they managed to bear the corpses up here was beyond me, until I learned later that the natives bring fibre ladders with them when they visit the cemetery. The heads of the mummies were propped up with arrows, so that the dead could sit here in their last resting-place and look down on the green landscape, the jungle, the hills and the villages where they had hunted, fought and lived.

10

The Chief with Twenty Murders to his Credit: The Initiation to Manhood

THERE was generally a happy, carefree atmosphere in our camp, which had gradually become the popular meeting-place and gossip centre for the natives. The only disturbing element was a family of wild pigs that used to keep the camp awake far into the night with their grunts and snuffles. Life in the camp started very early in the morning with the natives bringing their produce to barter with us for the much desired sea-shells. A swarm of laughing children would come and play, and by the time the sun had climbed over the eastern mountain-top, the camp was full of natives, all occupied in some activity or other. One boy, for instance, would be busy shaving the hair off his father's head with a bamboo razor; a man would sit beating a piece of bark with a stone to make it soft and pliable; the girls would be making grass bracelets or carrier nets out of strips of bark; an old man would be sitting with several children around him recounting legends of ancient times or of the tribe's exploits or his own prowess. It was an agreeable family atmosphere, and I gradually felt at home among these dreaded Kukukukus up in the green mountains.

I often sat with the headman, Momakowa, who, through

the interpreter, told me many details of the daily life of his tribe, and of the laws and ceremonies. He himself had five wives and, when I told him that white men had only one wife each, he looked very surprised; I detected a look of pity and disdain in his eyes. How a white man could manage with only one woman to work for him, he could not understand. It is true that many of the Kukukukus had only one wife; they, however, were the small fry in the community. Two wives was the average for a man of the world. Momakowa, who was thirty, had a splendid physique and was a famous warrior. He had taken part in many battles and was more than willing to relate the details of his numerous killings. For each victim he could recall he drew for me a line on the ground, and by the time his recital was ended there were more than twenty lines in the tally. There were others who filled in for me the picture of Kukukuku life: a garrulous old warrior, called Yagagaga, for example, and his wife Yambena.

When the time draws near for a woman to give birth to a child, she goes with other village women into the jungle, where they build a small hut and inside it make a couch of soft leaves. The men are forbidden to go near the hut. The women help her with the delivery and cut the umbilical cord with a bamboo knife, or simply bite through it. The birth takes place while the mother is in a kneeling position, holding on to the sticks in the roof of the hut. As soon as the birth is over, the other women leave the mother alone with her newborn baby; but if the child is deformed, they carry it off and throw it away in the jungle. When twins are born, one of them is killed and thrown away. The probable explanation of this is that, if the birth is not normal, the natives fear that evil spirits are present, and so to make the event normal they discard the malformed, or one of a pair of twins. When the women bring news of the birth to the village the father immediately goes out, with other men of the tribe, to shoot birds and possum, the most prized of jungle game, and if possible a pair of mountain kangaroos. On returning from the hunt, which may go on for two or three days, the father prepares a feast of meat and sweet potatoes, and sends for the mother, who then returns from the jungle with her new-born child.

The father himself must not touch meat for a month; everything he shoots or traps has to be given to the baby's mother, and as long as she is nursing the child, she does not have to prepare her husband's food. That is done either by his mother or by his sisters. She does not work in the fields either, to start with; but as soon as the baby is a little older, she takes it with her to the fields in a carrier net on her back or she carries it on her hip. When the child starts to walk it is given its first clothes, which consist of a tiny skirt of tapa-bark, if it is a girl; if it is a boy, he is given some strips of tapa to hang over his front and his behind. (This is done, by the way, not out of modesty, but to keep the flies away.) As soon as the child begins to understand what is said to him, he is given a name chosen by the father and the mother. The first part of the name is always the clan-name; the other part is some derivative of local life—a tree, perhaps, or a flower.

A girl child always goes to the fields with its mother, whereas a boy will hang on to the company of older boys from whom he soon begins to learn some of the things he needs to know later on in life. I have often seen a little pot-bellied fellow of three or four shooting with bow and arrows which his father or uncle or big brother has made for him; and it is not long before he goes hunting small game with the older boys, or playing war-games with them. He grows up fast. He observes the brutal realities of life; sees the corpses of the slain; helps, perhaps, to stone a prisoner to death and takes part in the subsequent orgies.

The most important event in the life of a Kukukuku boy is his initiation into manhood. As I mentioned earlier, I had, unfortunately, no chance to witness the initiation ceremony among the Kukukukus. The following description, therefore, is based on what the interpreter, Ingiham, and Momakowa told me. The ceremonies apparently vary slightly from village to village, but the basic rituals are the same. There are two stages of initiation: one at the onset of puberty, the other on its completion. The first phase takes place when the boy is between seven and ten, one factor being the convenience of initiating a fair-sized group of candidates at the same time. As a rule, there will be a group initiation, say, every second or third year. When the leading men in the village have decided which of the boys of the village are ready for initiation, and when the ceremony should take place, the boys' parents begin to collect food for a feast. All the boys' male relations go into the jungle, prepare a clearing and build two or three huts according to the number of boys to be initiated. No women may appear at the appointed place.

When all is ready the boys are led out from the village amid the lamentations of their mothers, these manifestations of grief being not so much spontaneous as a prescribed element of the ritual. The boys know very well that they are to suffer various ordeals, such as having their noses bored, but their misgivings are tempered by the knowledge that soon they, too, will display the outward signs of manhood. The boys are led to the huts, in which they will live for the next two or three months. The women of the village bring out food and place it somewhere near, but without showing themselves to the boys. They put down the food, call out and disappear as quickly as possible, after which a couple of boys go and collect the deposited rations. Some of the older men come out and stay for days on end with the boys talking to them about the obligations and opportunities of manhood. As a rule it is a boy's *amo*, or uncle (preferably the mother's brother), who instructs him in his future duties towards the tribe and the community in which he lives. Some of these preparatory lessons consist of practical instruction in sex behaviour; others are devoted to passing on to the boys the cherished myths of the tribe. During the night the boys sit with the men in the moonlight learning tribal songs dedicated to the moon. During one of these nocturnal sessions the boys may hear an uncanny sound, as of big, soft wings in motion. It is the *tumbu-lun* which the men swing around to keep off any evil spirits. At first the boys are not allowed to see the *tumbu-lun*, but later, when their noses have been pierced, they are let into the secret of how the strange sound is made, and they are told never to reveal it to a woman. Indeed, one function of the *tumbu-lun* is to keep the women respectful and submissive before a mystic power revealed only to men.

The whole of these preliminary proceedings are marked by a great solemnity; carefree childhood is over, and years of great import await the boys. Various rituals serve to impress this transformation on their minds, including many painful inflictions devised to plant these experiences in their memory. Various foods are forbidden the boys until, in three or four years time, they have passed through the final stage of the initiation ceremony. These deprivations aim to teach the boys self-control, and the most desirable and delicious foods, therefore, are on the prohibited list —such as possum meat, the appetizing fruit called *marita*, and a certain kind of sugar-cane. The boring of the noses takes place a few days after the boys move out to the huts. This ordeal gives a boy an opportunity to show that he can take pain without flinching. If he puts up a resistance, he is held down by two men, while another (often the boy's uncle) first rubs his nose with water, and then makes a hole in the gristle between the nostrils with the pointed bone of a bird. When the bone is withdrawn, a feather from the wing of a cassowary is put through the hole, a magic symbol supposed to ensure the boy the speed of a bird in hunting or fighting.

This operation concluded, the boys are taken to the nearest water-hole, where they are made to dip branches in water and whip each other in order to get rid of the woman-smell from their mother. When they return to the huts they find a small platform of bamboo has been raised, and on it three little heaps of the prohibited foods. Within sight of these tantalizing dishes they are now taught the various taboos and laws which in the future they must practise and obey, and in order that the instruction shall be remembered the boys are made to run the gauntlet between two rows of men armed with thorny sticks who beat the boys until the blood runs down their bodies. This running the gauntlet is not an expression of sadism; its psychological intention is revealed by the pride the boys take in the scars and bruises inflicted upon them. They carry themselves more proudly when they have been through this ceremony; they realize now that they are not children any more and must behave as men of courage and endurance.

The boys stay in this 'school' for another two or three months. Their wounds are treated with healing herbs and the cassowary feather in their noses is replaced by a stick of sugar-cane. They are given plenty of nourishing sweet potatoes, and they are permitted to go hunting with the men for wild boar, birds, lizards and rats—although these, too, they are not yet allowed to eat. The meat they take in these hunts is either hidden in a water-filled hole in the rocks, packed in wet clay by a rivulet, or smoked over a fire; it is being kept for the feast with which the first stage of the initiation concludes. When a sufficiently large store of meat has been collected, the boys return to the village. They are now dressed like men; they no longer wear a piece of tapa bark fore and aft, but a smart triangular kilt made of several layers of dried grass plaited together. Friends and relations from nearby villages are invited to a grand feast, where they eat, drink, play the flute and sing—without, however, making too much fuss of the novitiates. But the feast is designed for them and it gives them a distinct feeling of pride. Each boy is now given a new name to mark his transition from boyhood to manhood. The naming ceremony proceeds in this fashion: some of the meat collected for the feast is hung up on a long string in the village. The boys are placed before it in a row. One of the village elders calls them up one at a time, cuts off a piece of meat for the boy, and while he eats it, is told the new name chosen for him either by his father or his uncle. The fact that he eats meat while learning his new name no doubt symbolizes that the new name has entered into him and that he is now a different person from what he was before.

The second phase of initiation to full manhood takes place when the young man is old enough to get married. Once again the group initiates are taken to a place of ceremony in the jungle, again given instructions by the elders in their duties as tribesmen and warriors. They endure more painful ordeals, including the cutting of their foreheads with sharp feathers until the blood flows. After that, they are allowed to eat the three kinds of food—

salt-maker at work

An old woman daubed in clay brought a pig with which to buy back
the prisoner

She was sure we intended to kill her son and eat him

prohibited since their first initiation. The youths stay on in the jungle, and are not allowed to see women for three or four weeks. They are given further instruction, this time in arms and military tactics, and listen to tales of prowess recited by the acknowledged warriors of the tribe. Finally there is a great feast in the village. The initiated return from the jungle, painted with plant-dyes, dressed in all their new finery of bracelets and shoulder ribbons of plaited straw and sea-shells. Friends and relations from neighbouring villages take part in the feast, which goes on for several days until the food runs out. Even enemy tribes are permitted to view the feast from neighbouring hill-tops. There is a gentleman's agreement that no village is attacked during initiation ceremonies, and even hereditary enemies observe a truce for the duration.

The initiation rites of primitive people everywhere have in common the purpose of inculcating those habits of discipline and endurance which are essential for survival in the jungle. European missionaries who work among these people should be careful not to interfere too brusquely with these traditional ceremonies. There are many unfortunate examples of boys taken away from their villages and brought up in mission schools who develop into undisciplined creatures with no feeling of responsibility, who steal and commit other crimes which they would never dare to do in their own community.

To return to the Kukukukus. When, after the final ceremonies, the young men have been accepted as fully-fledged adults they are allowed to marry. In order to prevent in-breeding, it is customary to procure the bride from a neighbouring village or settlement within the tribe. It is the fathers, as a rule, who arrange the marriage, who indeed probably decided the match while bridegroom and bride were still children. When such a betrothal is arranged, the boy's family pays a certain proportion of the bridal price to the girl's parents, thus reserving the girl for her future husband. The price will be a pig or two, some stone axes or necklaces of sea-shells. The final price is not decided upon before the girl is actually marriageable, and depends on how she develops. If she remains puny her value falls, but if she promises to be a fat, strong wife who can give birth to many children and work well in the fields, she is highly priced. The respective family fortunes, too, influence the market price. A wealthy villager will not let his daughter go for a couple of stone axes and a few sea-shells. As the girl grows up her fiancé's father has constantly to deposit a little more towards the bridal price to keep the girl reserved. Sometimes there are long discussions about the price. The buyer complains of the girl's deficiencies in order to reduce the price, while the seller emphasizes her virtues and advantages. In these disputes the uncles often have to be called to reconcile the parties.

The Kukukuku girl does not go through any initiation ceremonies, but when she is mature at the age of thirteen or fourteen, her mother tells her the little she has to know, and the girl then moves to her future husband's hut and lives for several months with his family. The young man may caress the girl, if she is so disposed, but they are always under the parents' eye, and cohabitation before marriage is strictly forbidden. I got the impression, incidentally, that sexuality is not very pronounced among Kukukukus, as it is among many other primitive people. They do not seem to have, for instance, any erotic dances. If the girl does not care for the man her parents have chosen for her, she runs back to them, and they, with some reluctance, return the payment they have received for her. But if the girl is satisfied with the choice of her parents—and she usually is—she shows it by preparing a meal for her fiancé and bringing it to him as soon as she arrives in his parents' hut. Thereafter, the full price will be paid over to the girl's parents, and the young man (assisted by his friends) builds a hut and moves into it with his wife. When this is done a feast is prepared by the bridegroom's family; a pig is killed, and friends and relations of both families join in the celebrations. Apart from that, there is no other ceremony in connection with the marriage.

In general, Kukukuku ceremonies are few and uncomplicated compared with those of the other tribes in New Guinea, not only on the coast but also among the Kuman people in the highlands further west which I later visited. Ethnologically it was also a disappointment to discover no trace of artistic sense among the Kukukukus; neither in their huts nor their weapons nor their clothes was there any attempt at decoration. The only semblance of it was in the plaited grass ribbons which the women wear on their heads. The explanation may be that the Kukukukus are too busy fighting to have any interest in colour and design. *84617*

11

What do the Kukukukus Believe? Myths of Human Origin of Man: Of Sun, Moon and Stars

IT is difficult to get a clear picture of the religious beliefs of the Kukukukus. They have no totem figures or gods, and from their scanty rituals one is inclined to conclude that what they worship is merely physical strength. The strongest warriors rule the tribe, and tribal life is marked by fights, raids and murders. The less warlike are overshadowed by the fearless warriors who take the lead in battle and ensure the continued existence of the tribe. A people without a writing or a system of signs and symbols can only maintain its traditions, myths and beliefs by oral transmission from generation to generation. The content of such spoken communication will inevitably change as time goes on, not only in details, but also in its essence and interpretation. No two story-tellers will tell the story the same way. It was very difficult, therefore, to get a clear picture of the Kukukukus religious mythology, which deals mainly with the origin and fate of man, and with the sun, moon and stars.*

One of their myths about the origin of man goes something like this: in an approximation to Kukukuku idiom—

* Valuable research has been conducted in this field by Miss Beatrice Blackwood of the Pitt-Rivers Museum, Oxford. Published in *Folk-Lore* No. 3, September, 1939.

'A man made a field and planted potatoes. (In all their myths there is always assumed the presence of man, and if you ask them where these first men come from, they look at you as if they thought you were mad to ask such a stupid question.) So, there was a man who had a field and planted potatoes. A possum came and ate them all. The man and his brother came and saw that the possum had eaten all the potatoes. It was sitting in a tree. They pursued it, killed and ate it. They put the bones of the possum in a river and then went home. They slept for two nights, and when they came back they saw that the possum's bones had developed eyes, ears and legs, like a man. They went home again and slept two more nights. Then they returned and looked at the possum. He was now a real man. The possum-man came out of the water and made himself a bow and arrow. He stayed by the river a whole month. The two men from the village returned again to find the possum-man. He stood by the river. They saw him disappear into the water. One of the men went home and told his wife about it. She made a grass belt and grass bracelets for the possum-man. They went down to the river to look for him. There was no possum-man. A large tree had arisen in the place where he had disappeared. A strange sound came from the tree, like the song of many birds. The man cut the tree down with his stone axe. He then cut a big hole in the tree. Men and women came out of the tree. He chopped off some more of the tree and more men and women came out. He went on chopping and still men and women came out. They were all singing. All the women wanted a man. They each caught hold of a man and said: "This man is mine." The man who had cut down the tree gave them each a name and told them where to go and live. They all sang as they went off through the long grass. They built huts.

The women became pregnant and gave birth to children. They grew up—and here we all are.'

The Kukukuku philosophy was no more profound than this when it expounded cause and effect in myths about the sun and the moon. The sun came about like this:

'There was a long, long rope. The sun was a being who walked on the rope. A man came and saw it. He shot an arrow after this being. But it went on walking on the rope until it reached the sky. Here the being became a sun. When the sun goes down the moon comes up.'

And where does the moon come from? Well:

'A man sat by a fire. He had caught a big possum. He wanted to put it on the fire. The possum jumped out of the fire and ran up a tree. Its fur was still burning. Then it ran up still further and became a moon. It was a big possum.' (A possum always sits with its back curved, like a half-moon.)

Here is the legend about the stars:

'A man was cooking food in a big bamboo stick. The bamboo burst into many pieces with a bang, and the sparks flew up into the sky and became stars.'

The plants which the Kukukukus grow in their fields originated in this fashion: 'A long time ago some people killed a man and cut him into pieces. They cut off his fingers, his legs, his arms, and smashed his head. They spread all the pieces over a new garden; then they made a bonfire. The fire flared up. Then they went to their huts and stayed there. After some time they looked at the field. There were now bananas, taro, yams, sugar beet, and *kau kau*. They took these and went around to all the fields and planted them. There was enough for all the gardens. Since then we have planted all these things.'

Some of the Kukukuku legends were fables about goblins

and supernatural beings which kidnap women and children and can transform themselves into snakes and birds. They were not unlike Grimm's Fairy Tales. The Kukukukus also had stories undoubtedly based on real events, mostly about their favourite pastime of killing and eating their victims. These stories were always told by the older men when they sat at sunset around a fire in the village with an attendant flock of listening boys around them. To understand these tales one must remember that the Kukukukus distinguish two kinds of fighting. One consists of fights between the men within the same group of villages who have fallen out about something—a field, a tree, or a woman. If one of the men should get killed in such a fight, compensation is paid to the relatives in the shape of a stone club or a pig, a payment which ensures that the relatives will not take revenge and that the solidarity within the group is maintained. The other form of combat is more serious altogether. An enemy village or a remote settlement is surrounded and raided, and (if the attackers are not beaten off) all the inhabitants are wiped out.

The Kukukukus seldom attack during the night, but usually at the break of dawn. If there are any survivors of a raid, these will flee to their friends in neighbouring villages and persuade them to make a counter-attack. This is seldom difficult, for the Kukukukus as a rule do not greatly care what they fight about as long as they are given a chance to kill. Plain murder will always be revenged; years may pass, but it is never forgotten. A tribe which has an unsettled account of this kind must always be prepared.

Here is one of the battle stories which reveals the brutal mentality and persistent bloodthirstiness of the Kukukukus: 'A man went out alone to shoot a bird. He climbed up a tree. He waited for the bird to come and eat berries from a bush below. Then some men from a distant village came along, saw the man in the tree and shot him with their arrows. He fell down and they finished him off with their stone clubs, cut off his head, arms and legs and carried him off. The next day the friends of the man who had been killed went out to look for him. They walked and walked through the long grass and came upon the strangers who were about to roast the dead man, together with some *kau kau*. They hid until it was quite dark, then crept upon the strangers who were now asleep. They cut some stakes, and each man went up to one of the sleepers and thrust a stake through him. When day broke, they cut off the arms and legs of the dead men and carried them off singing as they went. When they came to their own village, all the people heard them singing and their wives and their children all heard them. The women cried: "Here come our brave men who have killed our enemies. They are coming now." The women put on their bracelets and necklaces and their new skirts. The men went on singing. They arrived at the village. They all sang. They cooked the meat on hot stones in the ground.'

Another war-ballad goes like this (with many repetitions omitted): 'Some men waking from sleep cried out: "Let us go and fight!" They took their bows and arrows and clubs and walked through the grass, chanting "Aia, Aia, Aia, Aia." They saw a man and shot at him with their arrows. One arrow went into his stomach. They cut open the stomach and removed the arrow. Another man hit him on the head with a club. Then they cut the arms and legs off the man and took them home to eat. They paid for the man they had killed with stone clubs and then they were all friends again.'

Practically all the Kukukuku stories are about killing. Occasionally they are plainly sadistic as, for instance, this

It was difficult to believe that these kind and friendly people were cannibals

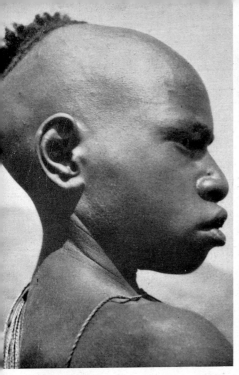

Typical Kukukukus from Kiwogwonga

They viewed my tape-recorder with suspicion

The boys wear a bird's quill in the nose to give them the speed of birds

Grief-stricken, the mourners daub themselves with mud and cut themselves with flints until they bleed

The mother's smoked corpse was treated as though she were still ali

one of some warriors who took the war-path to another village to revenge a murder. The story ends with this grim description: 'They lay in wait a long time. They saw a man leave the village. They shot him in the leg with an arrow; they hit him on the head with their clubs. Then they cut his stomach open. They cut off his sex organs and put them on the path so that his friends should find them. They cut off his arms and legs and took them home to eat. They sang on their way home to the village.'

Here is a tale of matrimonial tragedy:

'There were two brothers. One was married. The other was not. The one who was married, died. The wife of the dead man said: "I will marry you now," but the brother said: "No, I am no good. I have a disease. Go and find a better man." So she went to another man in the village. In the other village they made a big marriage feast. They collected food and made bamboo flutes and danced. The man who had declined to marry her put on his sea-shells and ornaments and went to the other village. He waited until it was quite dark. He went up to the fence surrounding the settlement with his flute. He wanted to take part in the dance. The people of the village called out to him to come in. He did. He played his flute and danced. The woman, his dead brother's wife, responded to his dance and said she still wanted him. She was hungry for him. The man she had just married now became furious. He shouted: "You did not marry the brother of your dead husband, you married me, and now you are crying for him." The woman took a stone and beat her head, as a sign of sorrow. She also took a stick and beat her dead husband's brother, who would not marry her, on his head. But the man took a stone and killed the new husband. They all shouted. Then he said to the woman: "Let us go." Then the woman and the man who at first had refused to marry her, returned to their own village. A long time afterwards, the man was killed by arrows and eaten by the men from the other village. One more man from either village was killed, so that two had been killed from either side. Then they were friends again.'

12

Salt from Plants: A Warrior with an Arrow in His Stomach: Tribal War halts the Journey

I BOUGHT a good deal of ethnographical material for the various museums for which I was collecting. One day a man came with two large bones on a string of bark tied round his waist, so that the bones hung on his belly. I bought them for a small knife and at once tied them round my own waist. The natives, who had gathered around, burst out laughing when they saw this, and told me that a man only wore these bones while his wife was pregnant and kept them on until she was delivered. I could get no exact explanation of why they were worn but, as far as I could make out, they served as a kind of chastity belt.

I found that the Kukukukus could extract vegetable salt from a certain plant which grows only in New Guinea; but other tribes in the island extract it from sulphur springs and sea-water. Normally salt is very much in demand by New Guinea natives when they are engaged in barter, but I had noticed that the Kukukukus were more interested in knives and in the small sea-shells called *giri-giri* which they strung around their necks and when, one day, I offered a man a handful of salt for a chain of wild boar teeth and he flatly refused to accept this as payment, I was surprised. Thinking he wanted a bigger 'price' I offered him two handfuls of salt, but the man was still not interested; he preferred a couple of small sea-shells. I became curious and called up the interpreter to inquire whether the man did not care for salt.

'I make it myself,' he answered, with a grin.

He proved to be the local salt manufacturer. His 'factory' was only an hour away, and I spent the next three or four days with him filming the whole procedure. Out-side the place where he made the salt grew some tall rushes called *pit-pit* (Lat.: *Saurania*). On chewing a bit of this plant I felt a decidedly salty flavour in my mouth. The salt-man cut some of the rushes and bound them into little bundles which he burned to ashes over a small fire. He next put these ashes into funnels made of the big leaves of the pandanus-palm with a grass filter at the bottom of the funnel. Then he slowly poured water through the funnels dissolving the minerals in the ash into brine which he ran off into hollow bamboo containers. These he placed on hot stones until the liquid evaporated leaving behind a thin layer of salt particles. It was a simple process yet one illustrating remarkable initiative for such primitive people. I tasted the salt. It was not as strong as ordinary salt and it had a coarse brown colour; yet it was, unmistakably, salt. It took three or four days to make a handful; yet the Kukukukus made it on a sufficiently big scale to be able to barter it to the other villages.

Every week we used to send one of the policemen down to the post at Menyamya to report our whereabouts and activities and to dispatch my films for development. It took three days, as a rule, for the man to get there and back; but one time the runner returned in record time with an alarming letter from the patrol officer, Bill Purdy, in Menyamya. It said:

'There is trouble and fighting among the natives in the western valley. So far eight have been killed. I need your men. Return immediately. Bill.'

We at once began preparations for leaving, and Moma-kowa was ordered to get carriers for sunrise for the next morning. A few hours later, while we were busy packing, there was another surprise. A heavily-armed warrior came to our hut with an arrow in his belly. We at once thought there had been an attack on the village and told the policemen to get ready for action. It turned out, how-ever, that the man had come from a friendly village a day's march distant. There had been fighting among the warriors of the village; no one had been killed, he said, but he had been wounded, and having heard that we had once or twice treated some of the natives for wounds he had now come to see if we could help him. The arrow had penetrated deeply and was broken off several inches out-side his body—and now, after twenty-four hours, the wound was septic and full of flies. We carefully removed the arrow and applied iodine to the wound. Apart from a twitch as the arrow came out and the iodine ran into the gash, the poor fellow took it very calmly. Oddly enough, we found he had no fever. We applied ointment and a plaster and off he went, he told us, to get on with the fight.

The next morning we set off, about half the village accompanying us as carriers as far as the village of Kiwogwonga. From here we pressed on with fresh carriers and spent the night in a couple of huts they built for us. I was sad at having to leave my friends in the village where I had lived for so many weeks. I had become fond of them, and had begun to get some insight into their manners and values. Their lives are completely different from ours; their modes of feeling and reasoning are unfamiliar. Their world of actuality is a savage and dangerous place where they must fight to survive, and where there are no checks upon their primitive and violent desires. Their other world, the invisible one, is alive with magic and mystery. When they can find no reason for accident, illness and death, they ascribe these misfortunes to evil spirits and invisible powers. Yet one cannot fail to be conscious of the fundamental human likenesses between these primitives and ourselves. The Kukukukus accept witchcraft and get drunk on murder, blood-lust and cannibalism; the white man goes to church or to the psycho-analyst or drowns his reason in drink. In the last few centuries while civilization has swept, like a tide, over the surface of the earth, over Africa, Asia, America and Australia, and has absorbed or obliterated the culture and behaviour of the old races of those continents, we often forget that those primitives, through thousands of years, had developed their own pattern of life, materially and mentally, to fit their environment. They found answers to their problems and riddles of living, answers which gave their lives a meaning and significance. We condemn their answers and their patterns. In a sense we are spiritual cannibals, devouring the alien and unfamiliar beliefs of the primitives and devouring, too, their strength and wealth by commercial exploitation. Such are the racial meditations and scruples which pass through the mind in a jungle camp. We are the cannibals, and we shall be punished for it, perhaps, some day.

13

Across the Mountains to a Dance: The Nose-boring Ceremony in the Jungle: Chased away by a Spear

THE little Drover tossed and climbed through the thunderclouds which lay thick over New Guinea's jagged mountains. I sat up with the pilot, Jack Shannon, who, pointing at a dark and threatening mountain range to the right of us said with a grin: 'You have to climb those to find the Morombo tribes.' I had chartered the plane to fly me into a remote district of the Highlands where the natives at this time of year celebrated the harvest with dance ceremonies. After a couple of hours' flight we caught sight of the American Lutheran Mission squeezed into a narrow valley between two wooded mountain-sides. About a mile from the Mission there was a landing strip and the little plane, circling like an eagle down between the steep mountain sides, landed neatly on the narrow strip where we were received by the missionary, Mr John.

It all started when my Kukukuku journey was cut short by an outbreak of fighting during neighbouring natives. I had flown back to Lae and from there planned a visit to the Kuman tribes in the Central Highland. At the Government Office in Goroka, I had asked the District Commissioner, Mr Downes, if he could tell me where the dancing ceremonies took place at this time of the year in the Highlands. Mr Downes passed the question on by radio to his various outstations, and from one of them he was told that the Morombo tribe were actively preparing for the annual harvest feast. But we should have to hurry, for the rains had come early this year, and the only available landing ground, the one by the Mission, would soon be closed because of the rain, for three or four months.

When, half an hour later, I said good-bye to Jack Shannon, he pressed one boot into the mud on the landing strip and frowned at the heavy rain-clouds.

'You'd better hurry your visit, for in a week's time it will be impossible to land here.'

I had been given a week to climb the mountains, locate the Morombo village, film and record their ceremonies. I was off next morning before light accompanied by four of Mr John's best boys, among them a guide interpreter called Maio who belonged to the Morombo tribe and knew their tracks in the mountains. As we had to climb most of the way, I had cut down my baggage to a minimum: film apparatus, recorder, sleeping-bag, air-mattress, tarpaulin, rain-proof cooking utensils, and some goods for barter, among them half a sack of salt, some tobacco and a bundle of old newspapers (which the natives used for cigarette paper).

For the first four or five hours we pressed steadily up open, grass-covered hills. Later the incline became steeper as we reached the timber line and the jungle where the ground and the tree-trunks were covered by a green, slimy moss which deadened all sound. There was a strange quiet among the lianas and the velvet-covered trees which stood like pillars festooned with thick foliage. Very little light managed to penetrate, and that was of a greenish hue. When a bird, on a rare occasion, flew up

Kukukuku warrior at his look-out

On the way to the mountain cemetery. In the background is Angu who
saved me by his presence of mind

The cemetery at the summit

The heads were propped up with arrows, so that they could see th[e]
villages and hunting-grounds

with a shriek, it sounded completely unreal. There was a light mist and everything gleamed and dripped with damp.

We stopped and listened to the stillness; in this absolute silence my breathing sounded in my ears like a hoarse groan, the pulse hammered in my throat, my ears, my temples. I was noise personified. Not until my heart and lungs had regained their normal rhythm was I able to sense the solitude here in the depth of the mossy jungle. We passed several streams. Over the first few the primitive suspension bridges were intact; higher up, the bamboo bridges had been swept away as they always are when the rainy season begins, so we had to wade across with the water up to our waists. Just before nightfall we had climbed to within a couple of hundred yards of the crest of the mountain, and there we made camp. The carriers quickly built a couple of huts of leaves and branches; we opened some tins and cooked some rice.

I felt completely exhausted after the day's climbing. My limbs, and especially my back, ached so much that I was afraid my old malaria, which I had caught in the Okawango swamps in South West Africa in 1947, and again in India in 1950, had been stirred up by the mosquitoes by the Lae coast, where I had stayed for a week before flying to Goroka. I lay on my air-cushion in the hut, so tired that I fell asleep with the food in my mouth; I woke in the middle of the night to find myself lying uncomfortably on my tin plate with some rice still on it. The fire was out, everybody was asleep. It was icy cold, a damp mist pervaded the hut, and I could hear the rain falling quietly on the tarpaulin over the hut. It was three o'clock in the morning, and as I could not get to sleep again I decided to rouse the carriers and start off right away. They were grumpy at being awakened before it was light, but after eating some fried *kau kau*, we started on our way just as the first light enabled us to see the trees and rocks through the mist.

In several places the mountain-side was almost perpendicular; we had to move with great care, for one false step would hurl us to death on the jagged rocks below. As the rain gradually increased the porters became more and more depressed, and their looks plainly told me that they thought it was madness to try crossing the mountains in the rainy season. I, myself, was soaked in rain and sweat, and at each step my head throbbed painfully with exertion and fatigue. At last we hauled ourselves to the top of the mountain, which we found enveloped in a thick fog; and here, seven thousand feet up, we rested for ten minutes. When we tackled the descent on the other side we could only see perpendicular cliffs disappearing into the fog farther down. We therefore kept along the crest of the mountain which in places was so narrow that we had to crawl along on hands and feet until at last we found a place where it looked possible to climb down. The descent was probably even more difficult than the climb up, and we were in constant danger of losing a foothold and crashing over a precipice. One of the carriers slipped, and as he did so his sack of rice broke loose from his back. We all stopped and stared at the disappearing sack which hit a rock and burst, the rice falling like a white cloud on the mossy-green mountain-side. We had lost enough food for several days. Shortly before sunset, tired enough to drop from exhaustion, hunger and thirst, we made camp. Deep down in the valley below we caught glimpses of huts through the mist. I swallowed some quinine and sleeping tablets and rolled into my sleeping-bag on top of the air-mattress in one of the huts.

In the morning I felt a little better, and the temperature seemed to be going down. The carriers were anxious to get on for they knew that in the village below there was a feast going on. For these feasts, which may last for three weeks, there are great preparations. The natives build long guest huts for the visitors from surrounding villages and store large supplies of food. I had expected a good reception, but when we arrived in the early afternoon it was evident that the Morombos did not care for my company. They had had little contact with Europeans and it also turned out that my interpreter, Maio, was not in the good graces of his tribe because he worked at the Mission on the other side of the mountains. When I entered the village square with my little caravan of carriers, all the women and children disappeared into the huts. There remained, in all, about a hundred men, in war-paint and feathers, sitting in groups outside the huts. They scowled at me with unfriendly faces. I asked Maio to take me to the chief, or *Luluai*, and to him I explained that I should like to witness the feast, and that I had brought him presents. The *Luluai* discussed the proposal briefly with the others and then showed me to a guest house on the outskirts of the village. I asked him to collect the old men of the village outside my hut and when they were assembled I gave them each a handful of salt which they earnestly licked. With the help of Maio I discovered that an initiation ceremony, including the boring of the boys' noses was due to take place; and on this I presented the *Luluai* with a large knife and told him that I had more presents for him, if he would let me attend the ceremony.

The rest of the day I walked about in the village in order to familiarize the natives with the sight of me; and after I had distributed various presents among them they seemed to reconcile themselves to my presence there. That night I retired to the accompaniment of songs and drums from the long guest huts; I was too tired to stay up for the performance. The next morning broke fine and sunny, and warriors from surrounding villages came streaming in, all magnificently decorated with coloured feathers from the birds of paradise, and many with their faces daubed with vegetable dyes, soot and boar grease. After sitting about over food and drink until midday, they began the ceremony. They stood in long rows, in the middle of the open square, half of them carrying snake-skin drums, the others clutching spears or bows in their hands. The dance which they performed consisted of hopping and stamping to the accompaniment of the drums, and as the tempo quickened they worked themselves more and more into a state of frenzy. The sweat poured from them and some of them shouted threateningly at me when I pointed my camera or microphone at them. Suddenly, there was an interruption. A group of young girls came yelling out of the guest hut, caught hold of one of the young men among the dancers and dragged him off, violently protesting, into the jungle. Through Maio I learned that this was a frequent occurrence during the dancing feasts. When one of the young girls takes a fancy to a man, she lets him see it; and if he ignores her overtures, she collects her girl friends and carries off the reluctant lover.

Next morning it was raining when the *Luluai* came to my hut and told me that I could attend the ceremony of boring the boys' noses. The five or six boys of ten or eleven who were to be initiated had been segregated in a hut during the night. They were now brought and off we went, in a long row, the initiates in the rear, towards the place several miles inside the jungle where the ceremony was to take place. As we went, the boys were made to force a way through the undergrowth and tall grass; the purpose of this was to test their physical strength and they were urged on in their heavy task by the curses and

He came with an arrow in his stomach, but went back to the fighting
again

A native of the Central Highlands with a head-dress of bark and shells

the compliments of their elders. At last we reached the appointed place: a small clearing by the bank of a stream. After some discussion, four of the men went to the stream while the others squatted some distance from them.

One by one the boys came out of the jungle and went, some of them a little hesitantly, towards the men by the river. There each of the boys in turn squatted in front of one of the men who held in his hand a small pointed bone and submitted to having the gristle of his nose, between the nostrils, pierced by the sharp bone. It was a painful operation, but none of the boys uttered a sound, though I could see them squirming a little. As soon as the bone was pulled out, each boy got up and held his head over the river, so that the blood could drip away in the water; they must get rid of their mother's blood which had gathered in them while they were in her womb. Afterwards the boys stood in a row in front of the men and each was given a piece of wild boar meat which had been brought along, wrapped in green leaves. It was all very much like the Kukukuku's initiation ceremony. Later in the afternoon, through pouring rain, the procession went back to the village, some of the men playing bamboo flutes. When we reached the village everyone streamed out gaily to meet us, the women and children gathering around the boys, each of whom now had a short piece of bark in his pierced nose. Fires were lit in the square, and soon the dancing and the drumming were in full swing. Many of the young girls, I noticed, now took part in the dancing, their bodies smeared with boar grease. As they danced, often very close to the men, there rose upon the air a penetrating odour of sweat and desire from their naked bodies. The glare of the fire was reflected from their excited eyes and on their white teeth and in the sea-shells and paradise feathers with which they were so liberally decorated. I was very late into my sleeping-bag that night.

I awoke next morning to find there had been a visitor in my hut during the night. My baggage had been ransacked, the sack of salt and all my other articles of barter had been stolen and most of my stores, except a couple of tins of coffee essence. Luckily my film camera and sound recorder had not been touched. I rushed angrily out of my hut and came upon a party of warriors stuffing themselves with my food. I kicked the tins out of their hands and shouted for the *Luluai*, but the chief was nowhere in sight. The warriors took on a threatening demeanour, and one of them threw his spear demonstratively towards my hut, a few yards from where I now stood. The gesture obviously meant: get the hell out of here, or else! . . .

I immediately told Maio to get ready to depart. While I was packing my precious films and recordings the *Luluai* shamefacedly came forward with some of the older men, apologized for the theft, and by way of compensation gave gave me a couple of *billums*—large carrier-bags—full of fruit and *kau kau*. I noticed as he did so that he had several of my stolen articles stuck into his bark belt, but I decided to say nothing; I was getting anxious not to miss the plane back. We started a little before midday, the only food I now had left being the coffee essence and the chief's *kau kau* and paw fruit—a sort of melon, but even this I was soon to lose, for at the first ford we waded through, most of the *kau kau* was washed out of its carrier net.

Maio was as pleased as I was to get away from the village, for he had been much chivvied by the inhabitants. We managed to get as far as the forest and build a couple of huts before the rain set in for the night. Next morning we ate half of the paw fruit and drank some cold coffee, supplemented by some wild sugar-cane which the carriers found. We emerged from the forest on to the bare chalk slopes where, as always, there was fog; fog so thick that we found it difficult to keep our bearings. Walking close to each other by midday we reached the top, but a couple of the carriers by this time were bleeding from cuts on their feet and knees. As I was bandaging their wounds I heard a scream behind me. In a split second I lifted my head and saw the head and arms of one of the carriers disappearing in the fog below me. A few seconds later there was a horrid crack followed by a faint wail. Maio called down to the carrier, a man called Lalak, that he must not move. The men fastened a rope round me and lowered me over the edge and down into the fog, where, on a ledge a few yards down I found Lalak with his legs dangling over the side and a bleeding gash on his head. He had apparently broken one leg, and was moaning in great distress. I called to Maio to bring down some blankets and more rope, and when these arrived Maio and I wrapped a couple of blankets around Lalak and bound his arms tight against his body. By the time we hoisted him up from the ledge he had lost consciousness. We massaged him, gave him cold coffee, brought him round and bandaged him as best we could. It was now raining again, but luckily we found not very far away a ledge under which there was some protection; and in this cheerless refuge we spent a sleepless night.

At first light, Maio and one of the carriers climbed down to the forest on the south side of the mountain to collect branches for a stretcher. When they came back a few hours later we had made a small fire and, for a change, some hot coffee. This restored Lalak, who had several times been near losing consciousness again. We tied the patient to the stretcher, so that he could not fall off, and started the descent. It was a slow progress, and several times we had to get the sick man, now delirious, over difficult ledges of rock. We moved so slowly that we had only got half through the forest when darkness fell. We managed to build a refuge, drank several mugs of cold coffee, and tried, in vain, to get some sleep. Never has a night seemed so long. In the stillness of the mossy jungle the raindrops sounded almost as loud as revolver shots.

The following day was the ninth since the plane had landed me. I was two days overdue, but it was impossible to speed our progress. We were worn out with hunger and, impeded by the stretcher, we could only advance slowly. Apart from that my fever was returning. Fortunately, the track was less steep; nevertheless, we fell several times and got some bad cuts, but were too exhausted to stop and bandage them. Every time we came to a stream we drank greedily, but still we went slower and slower. Every five minutes we had to take fresh turns in carrying poor Lalak who was now senseless for long periods on end. That night we slept in an abandoned hut. The last of our miserable stock of food was gone and we could find nothing edible in the fields; the wild pig had cleaned them up. We took turns keeping alight the small fire on which we tried to dry our clothes and blankets. The rain now streamed down worse than ever. I shook with fever, and hissing noises in my ears from all the quinine I had swallowed. We got moving again before daybreak, as none of us could sleep. Maio led the way with his torch, the rest of us close behind, and as it got light we caught a welcome glimpse of the Mission far below us.

Suddenly Maio shouted:

'Look, Master, balus balus!'

He pointed down to the landing strip, and through the misty rain I made out a white cross. It was the plane. I had given up all hope of being flown out of the valley and

I was now filled with panic lest the plane should take off before I could reach it.

On the veranda of Mr John's bungalow the missionary and the pilot, Jack Shannon, were having lunch. When I staggered up to them, I could think of one thing, food. I threw myself at the table and ate greedily while Mr John attended to poor Lalak. Jack told me that all the air-strips except Banz were closed by the rain.

'But,' he added, grinning, 'I arranged an emergency landing here on my way home from Mendi to see if you had got back. I have waited for over two hours, and we must be off at once. It looks like more rain.' He was just going to have a cup of coffee, he said. But not for me. I had had enough coffee. Half an hour later I sat in the little Drover again, almost looking forward to flying over the mountains, through which I had trudged the last five days. But before the plane had breasted the mountains, I slid into the sleep of exhaustion.

14

Love Ceremonies: Witchcraft and Superstition: The Motley World of the Spirits

THE landing ground in Banz could be kept open through the whole of the rainy season because it lay relatively far away from the highest mountains and had sufficient slope for the rain-water to drain from it, and here Jack Shannon put me down. As long as I wandered not too far away from Banz, I could be sure of returning to Goroka, and from there down to the coast. I felt much better after my sleep in the aeroplane, and I spent the night in a mission station near the landing ground. Next day I got hold of some carriers and walked about twenty miles along the Waghi river to the government station at Nondugl, where I had a letter of introduction to Barry Osborne. For the next six weeks I was always within two days' march of Banz. With the Nondugl station and the reconnaissance station of Minj on the other side of the valley as base, and with interpreters from there, I visited several of the Kuman villages in the district. The following description of the tribes' life and culture is based on my own observations and on information given by Barry Osborne in Nondugl and the patrol officer in Minj, Dougherty Jeffery; and a missionary in Denglagu, John Nilles, who had lived many years in the Central Highlands and who translated the Kuman songs.

It was the worst time of the year to spend in the mountains, for almost every afternoon and night it poured with rain. The natives did little work out of doors, but kept to their huts or huddled around a fire in the open, and the cold, wet weather depressed them, so that they were not always inclined to talk. I therefore bought half a sack of salt from Barry Osborne and doled it out to make them more communicative about the affairs of the Kuman tribe. They differ in many ways from the rest of the New Guinea natives. Their culture is on a much higher level than that of, for instance, the Kukukukus, and in spite of the fact that for many years they have been in contact with Europeans, their way of life, traditions and habits are, on the whole, unchanged, save for the fact that they have given up tribal wars and cannibalism.

The Kumans saw Europeans, for the first time, in 1933, when a party of Government officials and gold prospectors came through the Waghi valley on their way from Lae to Mount Hagen. The following year a Government station was opened. As the natives had never before seen white men, they were at first alarmed. They took the whites for supernatural beings, since all supernatural beings in their mythology were white. For two or three years after the setting up of the Government station, the Europeans had little influence on the natives, outside the immediate neighbourhood of the station, where they put a stop to the tribal fights and to cannibalism. Some time after the establishment of the station a party of Roman Catholic missionaries arrived from Madang to start a mission among the natives in Chimbu and the Waghi valley. Before arriving at the Chiambugla country from the Saghi valley, they had made friends with the chief of the tribe, Kawagl, who was known all over the district as an outstanding leader and, formerly, a very brave warrior. He led the mission across the mountains to Chimbu and Waghi, and everywhere they went in his company the missionaries were given a very friendly reception by the natives.

Two missions were established to begin with; and the natives visited these bases in order to sell their produce and to barter their labour for goods. Later on mission schools were set up at various points in the district. Everything looked settled and promising until trouble broke out suddenly. The natives burned a little school which had just been built in the Chibu valley, and when ordered by the missionaries to rebuild it, they refused. As a punishment the missionaries shot some of their pigs, an act which infuriated the Kumans. The following day two of the missionaries were attacked by armed warriors; one was speared through the throat, the other one escaped. A month later, in January 1935, the Kumans attacked another missionary farther down the valley and seized all his possessions. In the fight he shot one of the natives but was himself so seriously wounded that he died on the coast three weeks later.

After these events the Kumans in the Chimbu district became so aggressive that white men no longer dared travel through that part of the country. Then the Government stepped in, put the district out of bounds to missionaries, and set up a post at Kundiawa in the Waghi valley.

A police officer led a patrol to Chimbu to arrest the native who had killed the first missionary; and on his way came upon a pitched battle between two clans. Thinking they were about to turn on his party he opened fire and killed a number of natives on the spot. The rest fled. The next day the patrol arrived at its destination and took prisoner about thirty natives whom they took off with them to Lae or Madang. Another patrol similarly brought

native of Goroka: in features
nd adornment he resembles the
Red Indians

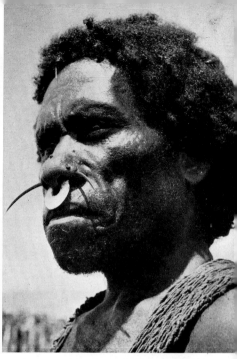

A Kuman tribesman

A suspension bridge of lianas and bamboo

The dancing takes place to the accompaniment of snake-skin drums

to book the natives who had mortally wounded the second missionary. After these punitive measures the natives in the Chimbu district began to behave more circumspectly towards the white man. At first the Government officials held the view that only force and physical punishment could secure peace and quiet among the clans, and every time the police received reports of a serious crime they raided the place during the night and took prisoners. After a short inquiry the innocent men were released; the culprits were put into prison for a couple of weeks and given corporal punishment before they were sent home. Although the reason for the punishment was always explained to the prisoners they remained puzzled why the white man should interfere with their 'private' affairs.

At last they became resigned to white rule, and the Government began efforts to establish friendly relations with the headmen of each clan. These men were called 'boss-boys' and were given as a mark of distinction a big, white glass ring to wear on their foreheads, a badge since replaced by a metal emblem. These boss-boys had to report periodically to the Government station upon any disturbances in the district and to bring in any offenders. The boss-boy system has now been replaced by the *Luluai* and *Tultul* system. For each clan the Government appoints a *Luluai* responsible to the local police and he in turn nominates his own assistants—*tultuls*—one from each subordinate clan. These men represent their tribe as a whole and are responsible for maintaining law and order in the district. Even the older, conservative tribesmen now acknowledge the greater security which the white man's laws have brought them. There is equal justice for the strong and the weak. They need no longer fear raids on moonlit nights; they can travel alone, far from their village, without risk of attack. The tradition that a crime within a clan must be solved by the parties involved still persists, however, although nowadays there is a willingness to accept pacific compromises. Thus a man who has been wronged will put up with an unfair decision because his adversary is stronger than himself, or tolerate a dubious decision because he has been threatened by witchcraft.

The presence of Europeans has modified the behaviour of the Kumans in other ways. The old stone axes, for instance, are disappearing and being replaced by steel ones; although now and then one still sees an old man using a stone axe to fell a tree or chop wood, and stone axes are still used at tribal ceremonies. Although fighting is forbidden by the Government, the Kumans still make weapons, such as bows and arrows, spears, battle-axes and shields, and the weapons are kept in the huts where they are always ready, in case . . . Bows and arrows and spears are, of course, still used in hunting and tribal ceremonies.

Let us take a closer view of these Kumans. Before us stretches a great valley dotted with villages and with fields and clearings laid out on the neighbouring hillsides, below the belt of jungle and forest. Higher up the mountains in the region of the Chimbu and Waghi valleys there are 60,000 to 80,000 people divided into twenty main clans. These again are divided into sub-clans composed of several villages each of which is, in effect, a large family group. A sub-clan is thus an association of families with its own songs and stories, its own feasts and ceremonies. Each sub-clan has a chief; a man of strength and authority who must, however, consult the older men of the clan about all decisions. Each village is a group of settlements where the land is cultivated by the women who grow the usual root crops, mostly sweet potatoes and vegetables. They also look after the family pigs. The men gather fuel, sometimes go hunting and organize the frequent ceremonies and feasts; apart from that they pass the time gossiping with each other. Each family settlement consists of several huts. One of these is a round, communal dormitory hut where the male members of the family sleep at night; there is also a smaller oblong hut divided in two, where men and women, separately, seek shelter during the day against the rain and the cold. Apart from that there may be one or more huts for the women.

The Kumans normally have only one wife, but there is nothing to prevent a man from taking an extra wife except that he must provide each wife with a hut and a field. It is a matter of prestige to have as many children as possible. The Kuman women, as a rule, dislike polygamy, and use violence, as well as witchcraft, to get rid of a rival. A wife is regarded as her husband's property. He is permitted erotic experiences outside marriage; she is strictly forbidden to do so without her husband's permission. If, with his consent, she receives payment for her sexual services to other men she must hand it over to her husband. But there is little sexual excess among the Kumans, even during their wild dancing ceremonies.

It was amusing to notice that the men who visited their wife or wives too often were grossly teased by the other men. The reason for this is that the men like to have as many children as possible so as to enhance their wealth and position and, according to the Kuman's belief, a man must sleep with his wife many times running in order to make her pregnant. They believe that the man, by these protracted endeavours, transfers the whole child to the woman's body. The women, on the other hand, are not at all inclined to have many children, so they take precautions or induce abortions. It is usual for young girls on marriage to receive from their mother advice and instructions about avoiding pregnancy for the first three or four years of marriage. They eat certain roots and leaves for this purpose and also repeat magic incantations which they believe to be effective.

When a child is about to be born the husband builds a little shelter near the woman's house. If the birth is difficult a witch-doctor is called to recite magic incantations as well as to give massage. Men must not be present at the birth but the mother's other small children are allowed to witness it and thus become familiar with birth from their earliest childhood. Here stories about the stork are not necessary. Two or three days after the birth the neighbouring families come to the mother's house for a little celebration. The father beaming with pride at what he believes is solely his achievement, kills and prepares a pig of which he gives the first portion to the mother. The second course is usually a sort of pudding made of bananas and sweet potatoes. A sorceress invited to take part in the feast touches the food with two sticks and recites a blessing which runs something like this:

Just as the birds, Marop and Yobai, fly hither and
  thither,
Just as Dangoma leaves heal a sore,
Just as Doru and the Kambia bananas grow well,
Just as the fur of a possum shines and the blue butterfly
  glistens in the sun,
So must the mother's and the child's body become alive.

When the child begins to talk, a little naming ceremony is held. The child is named after one of the older relatives, in whose lap it sits for the occasion. A medicine-man makes a ring of the leaves of a plant called *Wagnugl*, holds it over the relative and the child, then quickly undoes the knot of the ring and says, 'From now on we shall call the child

Watching a Morombo dance

The procession sets off in the rain for the nose-piercing ceremony

The men stood in rows and, after a preliminary rattle of their drums,
began to sing

so-and-so. You must take care of it and protect it.' The child and the relative after whom it is called will never use each other's real names, but will always call each other 'Dina,' which means same-name. Other names may later on be added, usually pet-names derived from plants or animals. Girls remain with their mother until they marry, but boys move over to the men's hut when they are seven or eight years old, and already at that tender age begin hunting small game and trying their hands at other manly duties.

When a boy is about ten he goes through the initiation ceremony. As a rule this happens within the family circle, but if there are several boys of the same village, due for initiation, the joint ceremony is held during one of the big village feasts, as it is also among the Morombos. The night before the nose boring is to take place, the young initiate sits with the men of the family in the men's hut and is schooled in his future duties and behaviour. He hears, for the first time, some of the myths of the clan and some of the men's cherished secrets. One of these is how to play the magic flute, an instrument like the *tumbu-lun* of the Kukukukus, used to strike terror into the women. The men of each family share one of these flutes. On this night of preparation the flute is played, outside the hut, by the boy's father or older brother; then it is brought in and explained to him, and he begins forthwith to learn how to play the family tunes upon it. It is impressed upon him that he must never show the flute to any woman. Women and children are told that the flute represents a large bird which lays its eggs on a great stone in the jungle, and if they should happen to see the *koa*, they would be struck blind, their bodies would rot and their pigs perish. If you ask the Kumans why they tell their women and children such a fanciful yarn, they reply:

'If we showed our flutes to the women, they would only laugh at us and they would refuse to believe that we control the guardian spirits with them. We should lose our authority, our women would no longer cook our food and tend our pigs.'

Next morning the boy is taken deep into the jungle, where the nose boring is performed in the same way as among the Morombos. The following day there is a great feast during which, on a given sign, the initiated boys come dashing on the scene with sticks through their noses, their bodies glistening with pig fat and painted in bold colours. They brandish their spears and bows with joyous shouts—and the feast is really on.

The girls, too, are initiated. At the first sign of maturity a four-day ceremony is held in the mother's hut during which all the older women of the family gather and tell the girl how to behave towards men and how to practise the basic laws of the tribe. On the final day a symbolic cleansing occurs after which the girl is considered adult. The women sit on in the hut far into the night and chant songs about the duties of women and the grandeur of nature. One of these songs runs like this:

Go and fetch water at the well, gather leaves and bring
    food.
Collect wood and warm the stones.
Put out the mats to sit on and the mats to eat from.
Men and women are coming, the children are gathering.
Let us make room for them.
Go up on top of the mountain Chmau,
See the beautiful forests;
Climb up the *Kundombo* and *gandia* trees,
See their white and red flowers in bloom.
See the birds alighting on the branch.

Listen to the songs when Kagl, Waugl and Dilu sing in
  unison.
They have all gone now, across the river and over the
  mountains.
There is a hole in the tree.
Go and see how sweetly the rainbow's child, the Oyie
  flower, hides itself.
Behold the lightning's and the thunder's children,
See how beautiful they are:
They live high up on the Pindaude heights.
Let them come down, we want to see them,
We want to get to know them and to hold them.

The woman who makes up such a poem is entitled to
royalties on it! If she leads the song, or teaches it to the
others for use on such occasions, she is given a present for
her work. The melody is always the same, but the words
may vary from village to village, especially by the substitu-
tion of local place-names.

Soon after the girl has been initiated, she looks around
for a suitable husband. Among the Kumans, it is, as a rule,
the girls who take the initiative in this matter and not the
men. The girls are already interested in boys at the age of
eleven or twelve, whereas the boys show no interest until
they reach the age of puberty. There are various round
games and ceremonies designed to get the young people
to know each other and to sort out potential marriage
partners. There is no question of a man buying a wife
against her will. There are two particular courting
ceremonies where the young people meet in this way. One
is a semi-private party called *Kango;* the other is a public
party called *Goanande.*

When a young girl gets interested in a young man she
invites him home to a Kango. If the young man accepts

the invitation, he goes to the girl's hut after dark, often accompanied by a friend, if it is the first time he has been to such a party. The mother is always present. After a brief introductory conversation, the two young people sit next to each other, holding hands. The boy then starts a song in a high-pitched voice and the girl joins in. They sway their bodies in time to the music and sometimes they kiss during these movements. The songs are traditional ballads in praise of nature, and sometimes, too, of human nature. When the song is over the young couple chat and laugh and, perhaps, start a new song. The boy may also recite a few magical love phrases to increase her warmth for him. Towards midnight the mother, who has been present all the time, will drop a hint that she wants to sleep. If the boy is tactful he will get up and go home. If he does not want to go, tribal etiquette forbids them to take further action and he can stay on until daybreak. If the mother finally drops off to sleep the couple may make love, although this behaviour is contrary to the rules of the tribe. Boys and girls can go to many parties of this kind with a new partner each time, and thus they gradually discover the one they like best. It sometimes happens that a couple meeting by chance during the day will start a *kango* in public, with a crowd of laughing and sympathetic lookers-on.

Kuman behaviour is altogether natural and uninhibited. When friends of the opposite sex meet, they do not greet each other by gestures or shaking hands; their greetings are much more intimate and thorough-going: they pat and stroke each other often in intimate places, accompanying their actions by affectionate phrases. Married men, too, indulge in *kango* parties, not with their wives but with other girls. The result, sometimes, is that they collect a new wife; sometimes the result is a brawl in which his angry

132

wife breaks up the *kango*. *Kango* time, for a girl, ends once she has married.

The other love feast, the *Goanande*, is arranged by marriageable young men and women from various groups within the clan. Boys and young married men equally take part, but the poor married girls are not even allowed to be spectators. The boys sit in a row, with their backs to the wall; the girls in a row on the opposite side, a girl opposite each boy. After a couple of songs, the boys move up a place so that they all get a new partner. During the session, which goes on all night, the boys have partnered all the girls several times and may have got to know them pretty well. A couple who feel specially attracted to each other can leave the party and set up a *kango* on their own.

The songs at the *Goanande* ceremonies are much the same as those sung at a kango party. They are always gay ditties: such as this—

> Where is the place we are going to sing about?
> It is here, the good place is here.
> Here where the binga and the kioya flowers grow on
>   the stone,
> Where leaves of yomga and dande trees glisten.
> What is the place down there called?
> It is called Kumbu Kamby down in the valley
> Where the Tirandie and Tarandie flowers bloom,
> Where the Bogonwan tree grows its ripe fruit for the
>   birds
> Which come over the river, over the mountains. . . .

Each song begins and ends with a chorus which serves to emphasize the melody.

When a young man has participated in several *kango* and *goanande* feasts, and has chosen (with her consent) the girl he wants to marry, he asks his father or elder brother to kill a pig and give it to the girl's parents. After that the young couple are considered engaged. The night before the girl moves into the young man's family, there is a farewell party for her attended by her relations and those of the man she is to marry. Wearing no bridal finery the girl sits in the middle of the circle of guests, while the women perform a ritual cleansing of her body. While this is going on the girl may sing a song, such as:

My father and mother, come and hold my body.
My face is hot, it burns.
It glows like the feathers of a Kawagl bird.
Father and mother listen to me, my skin burns.

Or the guests may sing one to the girl:

As the Boma and Dangoma plants grow together,
As a man calls for his dog and it quickly comes,
So you two shall go together. . . .

A couple of days before the wedding ceremony some of the girl's male relations visit the young man's home to inspect the presents he has collected for the girl's family: stone axes, steel axes, jewellery made of sea-shells, and one or two pigs, which will be killed on the wedding day. If they find the presents sufficient, they discuss what presents the girl's family will supply, partly on the wedding day and partly in the future. The exchange of presents is thus a token of unity between the two families. On the wedding day the young man goes with his family to the girl's home bringing the presents and the pigs that are going to be slaughtered for the feast. The presents of both families are laid out in two heaps in front of the girl's home. The wedding ceremony now proceeds. On one side of the presents the young girl and her family stand together; on the opposite side stands the bridegroom's family. The bride's father or uncle calls forward a man and a woman from the groom's group, and these go over to the girl, take her by the hand and lead her over to her husband. By that act she has left her family. The two young people are now man and wife. Then the pigs are slaughtered, and a riotous feast is held.

Among the Kumans present-giving is frequent and popular. Generally the exchange of presents is a token of friendship between persons or groups; but even within families there is a constant exchange of presents between a man and his parents or his in-laws. It is always assumed that the presents exchanged shall be of equal value. Presents are also 'lent' to a young man so that he can put up a good show for his wedding or to show sympathy in case of death or illness. If a man is offered a present of such value that he has no immediate hope of returning one equally good, he may not refuse it. That would be a deadly insult to the donor. A mean man who never gives presents has no friends, whereas a man who habitually gives presents of higher value than the ones he receives is highly esteemed in the village.

Presents are expected and given, as we have seen, for immaterial things such as songs and stories. There are in every clan men and women of surprising imagination and good memory, who, in this way, amass substantial wealth by singing and telling stories. The story-teller knows the names of every bird and plant in the neighbourhood, and has an encyclopædic knowledge of the traditional laws of the clan. Presents are given, too, as a form of compensation; in requital of an oath or an insult. If a woman, in a fit of anger, destroys some of her own property, she can demand compensation from the person who infuriated her.

Life among the Kumans is richer in songs, stories, feasts

and ceremonies than among the Kukukukus. Their greatest feast, called *Bogla Gende*, occurs every five or six years, and as it is a feast for the whole tribe it attracts audiences of several hundreds. The preparations alone take almost a year. The two initial ceremonies are, first, selecting the pigs for the feast and, second, giving the pigs the first of many special feeds to fatten them up for slaughter. The men prepare the food and the women give it to the pigs, saying: 'Eat this quickly, get fat and heavy. We are already playing the flutes to celebrate your coming slaughter.' New clearings are made so as to grow enough food for the feast. The men fell trees in the jungle to build three guest houses, often one hundred yards long, one for the men of the clan, one for the women and children, and one for guests from other clans.

As soon as the houses are ready and sufficient food gathered, the dancing starts: the big killing of pigs does not take place until the dances have lasted four weeks. The dances are marked by stamping and rhythmic swaying of the bodies to the accompaniment of songs and drums. Several of the men take turns in setting the pace and singing the ballads, which mainly describe everyday happenings. A man's prestige depends very much on how he leads the singing and sometimes he even pays his friends to applaud him.

The dancing begins quietly enough; but after an hour the sweat pours off the dancers, the drums beat faster and faster, and the performers reach a condition of ecstasy. Various families take turns in dancing and keep it up for hours a day for five to seven weeks. The climax of this protracted affair comes when the pigs are slaughtered, and the orgy of eating lasts several days, after which everyone goes home, replete and exhausted. The sequel is often a prodigious hangover, due partly to the consequences of eating too much bad meat and partly also to the emotional exhaustion brought on by the prolonged excitements of the dancing. Family and tribal disputes are often traceable to these excesses.

The annual Harvest Festivals are quieter celebrations. A village gives part of its crop of sugar-cane, bananas or nuts to another village which, for this consideration, provides the festivities; the next year the rôles are reversed. A third big feast, very similar to the *Goanande* ceremony is the one called *Ambuingu Beglkua*, which means: 'the women break into the men's house.' This feast, which occurs every third or fourth year, begins with the young girls gathering, during the night, outside the house of the men of another clan. Singing the usual *Goanande* songs the girls, in couples, enter the hut where the men await them and sit down by the wall, each opposite a man. After a song session, like the one at a *Goanande* feast, the rest of the night is devoted to love-making. If a girl refuses to take part, she is sent home. During the day both the men and the girls dance outside the men's hut to the accompaniment of drums, and from time to time couples break away and start a *kango*. These romps generally last four or five days and end with a substantial feast provided by the men.

The purpose of this ceremony, in which the usual rules of the clan are in abeyance, is no doubt to dispose of the unmarried girls. The Kumans have no use for old maids. Every mature woman is expected to have intercourse with a man; and a widow is disposed of to a fresh husband as soon as her period of mourning is over. The only bachelors in the clan are the feeble-minded or deficient. If a man becomes impotent he lends his wife to a clan brother in order to procure an addition to the family.

Kuman women, like most primitives, are dominated

by their men; yet they are far from being defenceless, and have much more influence than one might expect. Their gossip about village problems and politics is often an important factor in determining the decisions of the clan. There are certain significant peculiarities about the relationship between the sexes. Ignorance of human physiology leads the Kumans to believe that women are dangerous to men during menstruation (although this does not apply between husband and wife) and a woman can use this supposition to revenge herself on a man who has angered her. She can step over his food, or brush it with her clothes, thus infecting it and causing illness in the man who is eating it. Anything a woman touches or steps across during this time is thereby considered unclean and dangerous: tools, building materials, food or firewood. A man seldom sits down where a woman has just been without first rubbing the spot with some leaves or a stick. A woman is also an offence to men when she is going through the menopause, and if at that period she is seen by a man washing herself in a brook, she must give him a pig for having inconvenienced him in this way. In earlier times she might even be killed for this unconscious offence. At parties the men and women always sit in separate groups. A woman badly treated by her husband has been known to hang or drown herself in revenge, thereby not only putting the man in jeopardy of evil spirits, but also requiring him to pay her family a substantial compensation.

Spirits and invisible powers play an important part in the life of the Kumans. When they are faced with problems they cannot explain, such as illness, madness, death, failure of crops and accidents they seek refuge in the world of fantasy and magic. They distinguish three categories of magic. There is, first, the beneficent magic which gets results, such as a love incantation which wins a wife or husband, or keeps the partner from infidelities. Another magic of this kind is practised by old women who claim to be able to produce boy births. The witch collects some plants with small roots resembling the male sex organ, and over these she croons an appropriate rigmarole as she feeds the plant to the pregnant woman. The mother must then sleep for a month with her head on a small bow and arrow so that she can dream her child into becoming a boy. Some witches declare that this magic is infallible in its results. Nearly all the planting of the fields is accompanied by magic invocations. They call upon the sun (they call it *Yaglvano*, which means Old Man) when the piles of a new house are put down to ensure warmth and prosperity for the house. The moon is looked upon as a female being and is called *Avamo*, which means Old Woman, but it is not worshipped.

Any strange occurrence, such as a bad dream, lightning hitting a tree near a man's hut, a lizard suddenly touching a man—all these things are thought to be omens of bad luck, which must be offset by magic of the second category, the protective magic called *Binga*. The word means rope and signifies a special kind of rope employed to draw evil spirits out of the body. Kumans seldom leave their village without wearing some kind of protective magic. Children are considered particularly susceptible to malignant spirits and are customarily provided with amulets round neck or ankles. When a man suffers from headache or fever, the medicine-man prescribes some pieces of bark from a tree called *Ombu*, and murmurs a spell while the patient eats. The bark has a slightly bitter taste, rather like aspirin; and it is not impossible that, magic apart, the remedy has a real remedial value. But magic is regarded as the real healer and in cases of nervous disturbance, caused by fear of evil spirits, the belief in the magic may well be a potent factor in the cure.

The third kind of magic is a malignant one called *Kumo*, an affliction of an hysterical kind, brought on by fear and fancy. *Kumo* is, of course, not identified in these terms by the Kumans who regard it as a witchcraft which kills by non-physical means. Old men and women who have been slighted are often believed to revenge themselves by *Kumo*. It can be inflicted without leaving evidence by an old man or woman who creeps round the village by night, and all stealthy, nocturnal walkers are suspected of dealing in *Kumo*. Strange as it may seem, this dreaded magic nevertheless can help to maintain peace and amity in a village, for no one is inclined to be unfriendly to anyone else lest the person who feels offended should, in revenge, invoke magic against the offender and precipitate illness and bad luck. In this sense the fear of *Kumo* produces a useful power of appeasement in village affairs.

If, however, a quarrel cannot be made up in spite of discussion and compromise, it may be necessary to resort to combat. The weapons in such mass duels are sticks and stones, and a fight may last for several days, with intervals, until too many of the combatants are wounded or exhausted to leave a quorum. If the battle fails to yield a settlement of the quarrel, then the last resort is a reconciliation feast at which compensations are exchanged between the parties.

Apart from invisible magic, there are also (the Kumans believe) real spirits around them, disembodied beings who observe and judge all human actions and, in this sense, take the place of what civilization knows as conscience. When the native steals or lies or inflicts cruelty, he has no sense that he is doing anything morally wrong; as long as there are no painful consequences, the Kuman mind is not troubled by what he does. If, on the other hand, some deed he has done is followed by bad luck, he believes that the spirits are displeased with him. He will then admit to himself that he has done wrong and is ready to atone by apology and compensation.

Accidents, too, are commonly attributed to the vengeance of evil spirits. The spirit world of the Kumans is abundantly populated. There is first the spirit *Kangi* which lives in the shady banks of rivers, and sometimes assumes the shape and clothing of a man. It slaughters pigs during the night and eats them; it kills men and women who make love out of doors. If the Kangi gets into a house, it is chased out by a medicine-man who then plants a little row of sticks in front of the hut as a warning to the spirit not to molest the hut again. There is another spirit, *Yogondo*, which lives under great stones in remote places, and can embody itself as a bat. It flaps around at night and steals produce from the fields, and its hoarse screech, ka-ka-ka, used to be considered a signal of attack. But nowadays the Kumans do not fear the *Yogondo:* they catch and devour all the bats they can eat. Two other spirits, *Barre* and *Tange* frequent swamps and lakes; they, too, can take on human shape, sing weird songs and threaten people with bows and arrows. The *Poglo* and *Kaiyange* spirits are also unfriendly and mischievous, and specialize in luring men and women to death in lakes and rivers. In the darkest shadows of the jungle live two other spirits *Dove* and *Dugl Baglkua* which can transform themselves into young men and have a habit of slaughtering pigs with their stone axes. If there is a disturbance among the pigs, then these spirits have stampeded them; and to ward off further attacks from spirits, the owner kills a small pig and flings some of its flesh into the dark shadows of the jungle. In return the spirit will, from then on, protect all the owner's pigs. The sacrifice is not wasteful, for the owner eats the rest of the pig himself!

The religious life of the Kumans is dominated by ancestor worship. They believe in a life after death, where the spirits of the dead live on, and retain the power to interfere with the living. They see how, in the course of nature, plants, animals and human beings come to life, grow to maturity and disappear again. Death is a transformation, not an extinction. When someone dies, the personal spirit, the *Kuia*, of that individual survives, and indeed for a considerable time remains near the grave of the departed. When a man dreams, it is because his *Kuia* has temporarily left his body and gone to visit the places the man dreams about. The belief that the dead continue their existence in another form is exemplified in the funeral rites of the Kumans. Immediately after a man has died, the corpse, daubed with grease and decorated with shells, is put on a rough bier and exposed in the village square. The relatives, smeared in mud and clay, sit by the body holding its hands and feet and howling and lamenting loudly to convince the dead man's *Kuia* that they grieve for his departure. The women mourners, especially, show no restraint in their mourning; they beat themselves with stones until the blood flows, cut off their ear lobes and break their fingers. The mother of a dead child will go so far as attempting to drown or hang herself. A mourning rite sometimes precipitates a bloody quarrel. If, for instance, a young married woman dies in childbirth, her relatives arriving for the funeral may be so overcome by grief and fury as to attack the husband and his relatives for allowing a member of their family to die.

The mourning rites generally occupy two or three days, even though the body is buried the first day. The corpse is put into the family grave, outside the village, in a sitting posture, with the legs drawn up. All but the face is covered in leaves and on top of the grave are placed sticks, leaves and pieces of bark covered by a thin layer of soil. Some Kumans even put flowers on the grave, not a usual practice among primitive people. If the dead person is a child, a boy, for instance, who has just been initiated, his family keep him sometimes for months before burying him. Even then they place the corpse in an open grave or in a hollow tree-trunk so that the corpse can still be seen, and not until the flesh is rotten do they bury the skeleton completely. The actual funeral itself is conducted by the male relatives who, when it is over, throw water over themselves and leap through an open fire so as to free themselves of contamination by the lurking spirits. For a long time after the funeral, the *Kuia* will hover around, not only by the grave, but also near the family's house. The buzz of an insect near the grave, or the sound of a rat or lizard scuttling in the hut during the night, may be signs from the dead. After a time a man's *Kuia* will hide in a lake or water-hole, whereas a woman's will slip down a rat-hole into the ground. But the *Kuia* keeps on returning to guard the family, to watch that traditions and rules are strictly kept, to punish the wrongdoer and reward the good. Its influence exceeds that of the living, for it can see all. A *Kuia* can even revenge itself on someone who has injured it in life.

Thus did the lives and customs and beliefs of the Kumans unfold themselves to me like a misty landscape. Through the long and difficult talks I had with old men and women in their dark huts, often while the rain poured monotonously down, the mist lifted, bit by bit, and the details began to reveal themselves. I almost began to visualize the spirits myself, and to feel them hovering around me when, after a whole day's conversation, I returned late at night to my own hut. It was difficult at times to endure the incessant rain, the vermin and the squalor as I tried to make the interpreter's language into a coherent pattern; yet it was with regret that I finally said good-bye to the Kumans, to fly back to the coast again.

Apart from the ugly episode with the Morombos I never encountered any deliberate malice among the natives. Often when I was labouring up the steep, slippery paths with my carriers, someone would slip, but the other would always wait to see if the victim had injured himself before they broke into their usual laughter. Once my three carriers, one of whom was the interpreter, played a little joke on me. When we crossed the mountains they often produced resounding cries which rolled in echoes over the landscape and announced our arrival. I imitated these cries and when I got far ahead of the carriers, which often happened on our way home, we kept contact with each other in this way. One wet afternoon I had got far ahead, but could still hear, from afar, their familiar cries. We were all wet, tired and hungry, eager to get home. Suddenly, their cries stopped. I sat down to wait for them, but fifteen minutes passed without a sound or echo from them. I began to get worried, and started back to look for them. At that moment there was a shout of laughter just behind me. There they all stood shaking with delight at their prank. They had taken a short cut, and for the last ten minutes had been standing stock still behind me enjoying my anxiety and my unreciprocated cries. That little episode cheered me. It was an impulsive expression of intimacy and confidence between us. We could have fun together. Life was again worth living, even though hunger gnawed at my vitals, and the rain poured down. We went on yodelling together and there came to my mind the song of the spirits:

A Kuman girl wearing a piece of shell as a brooch

The volcanic island of Manam

The girls dressed in banana leaves, began to da

Our song shall reach as high as the top of Mauge and
   Waiya,
It shall go over the Kuglbagl and Darua mountains,
As far as to Numbu and the Maugl valley shall it be
   heard,
Even though we stay here, our song shall go on.

15

A Happy Man with no Shirt: Twenty-four Hours on Paradise Island: The South Sea Girls Tickle Our Chins

In the Bismarck Sea, north of New Guinea, lies a small group of islands, mostly of volcanic origin. On the map they appear as black dots, and only the largest of them have names; but one of those nameless dots represents for me the realization of a dream which I share with most people: the dream of visiting a tropical South Sea island, inhabited by kind and happy natives, where there are a profusion of fruit and an ideal climate of sunshine and cool breezes blowing through the palms . . . that paradise is Manam Island. I got there by a lucky chance. During a couple of days rest in the guest house in Goroka, where I had gone after my stay with the Kumans, I decided to fulfil a long-cherished wish to sail up the Sepik, the largest river but one in New Guinea. I had acquired a fresh supply of films and, with a bit of luck, I could manage the trip before the rainy season began in two months' time. I had first of all to fly to the little coastal town of Madang, on the north coast, and for the moment all air traffic from Goroka was stopped because of rain and mist. For two days I sat in the Control Room on the landing ground together with a couple of stranded pilots and waited for the all-clear. One of the pilots, Bill Parsley, was from

Madang, and was returning there with a plane-load of sacks of coffee from one of the plantations around Goroka. On the third day we got permission to start. Bill threw out a coffee sack to make room for me, and after circling the airfield we set off for the 10,000-foot mountain range to the north.

'I hope it isn't wearing its hat,' said Bill, 'otherwise it will be expensive coffee if we don't get across today.'

It was a chartered plane, and the coffee planter had to pay for each day it was held up. Unfortunately, the mountain was wearing its hat, an exceptionally wide hat of white cumulus cloud which blotted out the pass we had to slip through. We circled round for half an hour making a few optimistic dives into the clouds in the hope of finding a hole; but the barrier of cumulus was unbroken, and at last we gave up and flew back to the Goroka valley. Here we were told that a Tiger Moth had just come through from Madang. The rainy seasons are curiously distributed in New Guinea: North, South, East, West and the Central Highlands all have completely different rainy seasons. Within 500 or 600 miles you fly from a rainy belt into hot sun and a cloudless sky. In Madang it was dusty and parched, people were sighing for rain. The District Commissioner in Madang, Mr Elliot Smith, who had just been appointed from Port Moresby, was willing to help me plan my trip up the Sepik river.

'As far as the climate is concerned, it is hell,' he warned me. 'I have never been there myself, and I should love to go with you. But when you are running a District it is the end of "going bush".'

He wirelessed to the District Commissioner at Angoram who sanctioned my use of the police post there, 100 miles up the Sepik, as my base. From Madang it was about 150 miles to the mouth of the Sepik. While waiting for a boat going that way, I bought various goods for barter in the Chinese town: fish hooks, nylon fishing lines, matches, sticks of tobacco, cotton material, coloured plastic bracelets and the like. I liked Madang with its prolific jacaranda trees. The few hundred white people there lived a placid life in a climate hotter than Lae. After a week I got away. A motor boat was going up to the Government post at Angoram to take supplies and to bring back crocodile skins. At the landing-stage I was introduced to the skipper, sixty-five-year-old Johnny Young, a fine character of the old school. He was the only total abstainer in New Guinea, a fact which betokened exceptional will-power. He neither wore nor possessed a shirt and always went about in shorts and sandals. He was as unostentatious in his language as in his dress.

Skipper Johnny was a wealthy man. He had made a fortune by disposing of American war surplus, and now lived a carefree life as one of the happy vagabonds of the South Sea. His thirty-foot motor boat was the best along the coast. Once in a while he accepted a cargo of freight, if its destination happened to be on his route; otherwise he wandered about the islands and up the rivers along the coast, did a little crocodile and duck shooting, traded a little with the natives and used his time as he pleased. He was a familiar and popular figure wherever he went. Apart from a couple of native boys, he had a white crony of similar tastes, forty-year-old Tom, whose only duties were to keep the diesel engine in trim and to keep Johnny company.

In the soft violet light of early morning, we sailed out between the coral islands of Madang bay and followed the coast west. It was very hot, though the breeze made the boat bearable. Dolphins leapt around the bows of the launch as if to demonstrate their superiority over our speed.

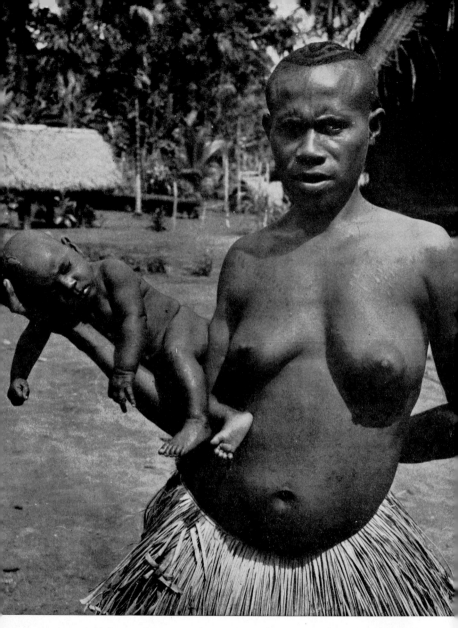

A baby on Manam Island has its midday nap

The women on the island have fine harmonious faces and move with
the grace of gazelles

In the late afternoon we anchored in a lagoon off a coconut plantation in Dugumur Bay, where the natives at once came out to us in their canoes and took us ashore to the plantation manager's house. He was a former Sydney business man and offered us ice-cold drinks, showers and dinner—and further cold drinks. But ice water only for the teetotal Johnny.

After this pleasant visit the natives rowed us back by torchlight to our boat, which lay a hundred yards from the beach. About midnight a strong wind got up across the lagoon, and we were roused by the boat banging itself against a coral reef. We started up the motor and tried, in vain, to get clear. We shouted for assistance to some natives sitting around a fire on the beach, but our cries failed to carry above the noise of the surf, and as neither Johnny nor Tom were good swimmers, I was the one who had to go over the side. I took with me a strong floorboard as protection against the sharp coral, and with this under me rode the surf to the beach. Once or twice, every time my feet touched coral, I thought of the jaws of a shark. There were many of them about, but I hoped they would not venture into the surf in a storm. In five minutes I was ashore explaining to the natives that we needed help to get the boat clear. They came off in a couple of canoes, and leaping up to their chests in the water manhandled the boat free of the reef. Several times the waves burst right over their heads, but they grinned and treated the whole thing as a joke. With the canoes in tow we sailed to the other side of the lagoon and anchored there in shelter. The natives, to each of whom we gave a stick of tobacco, disappeared happily in their canoes in the direction of the plantation. Thanks to them this diversion on the reef only cost us a couple of hours' sleep. But I was kicking the rest of the night, dreaming of sharks snatching at my feet.

We left the lagoon before first light. The wind had died down, but there was still a heavy swell. After a couple of hours we caught sight of a dark triangle on the horizon.

'That's Manam,' said the Skipper; 'my little private South Sea paradise.'

The triangle was growing in size, and I could see smoke rising from it.

'It is a volcanic island, and it is always smoking, day and night,' Johnny continued. 'Sometimes it emits rings of smoke at exactly five-minute intervals. It is 6,000 feet high, and has only been climbed by one man, an Englishman studying volcanoes in the Pacific. The natives on the island dare not approach the volcano for there are gods up there, you see!'

As we approached the island, five or six men in out-rigger canoes came out; some of them jumped aboard and let their canoes be towed. By the time we anchored some yards off-shore, the boat was surrounded by happy, shouting natives, swimming and paddling. Their canoes are made of hollowed-out tree-trunks with a small out-rigger to balance them in rough seas, and on the stern are carved heads of the gods who protect the boats and ensure large catches of fish. On the beach a crowd of women and children had gathered to greet us with cries of Ai, ai, ai! Their pleasure was evidently keen, for boats rarely visit the island. We distributed presents of fish hooks and lines; and in exchange they filled the boat with all kinds of fruit: bananas, oranges, coconuts, paw-paw fruit, pine-apple and galip nuts.

'There is a fabulous wealth of fruit in this little island,' said Johnny. 'Every time I come here I load to the water line with fruit. Give them a small fish hook and you get fifty bananas back.' He climbed into one of the canoes, with his gun, and went off duck shooting up the coast.

Tom and I went ashore with my camera and sound recorder, to see what we could film on this enchanting island. The moment we stepped on shore, we were surrounded by laughing, gesticulating women and children, who tickled our chins by greeting. It is a method of greeting between the sexes which I would not willingly introduce into civilization! With a train of children behind us we went up to the village, a few hundred yards inside the jungle, which grew all the way up the mountain-side, and consisted largely of coconuts, bananas and pandanus palm. One of the young men who came with us spoke very good pidgin-English. He said his name was Lao and that he had worked on plantations on the coast and in the warehouses at Madang. He was obviously keen to show his friends that he could speak the white man's language, and whether for that or for other reasons he seemed to have a good standing in the village.

The village consisted of a long 'street', flanked by two parallel rows of huts on piles. Unlike most of the primitive huts I had seen in New Guinea, these had square openings to serve as windows. Their floors were two yards above the ground and a small ladder led up to the entrance. Below the huts was kept the fishing gear, and here, too, their big, black kanaka pigs lay in the shade. Each hut consisted of one large space where the whole family slept on the floor on mats of banana leaves.

Our entry into the village caused a sensation. Both Tom and I were dressed only in shorts and shoes, so that our white bodies showed very distinctly among the black ones. From all the huts women and children came tumbling out to greet us, and even the old women climbed laboriously down the ladders to come over and tickle our chins. The reception was so hearty that it gradually became a bore, especially when some of them, in their eagerness to acclaim us, put their dirty fingers into our mouths. But they were very kind. Many of them brought bananas, oranges, coconuts or galip nuts in such quantities that we had to recruit the children to act as carrier for the gifts.

To secure some peace from these curious and generous women, we finally took refuge in the men's communal hut. Here sat a few old men mending their fishing tackle. Through the door of the hut I could see the peak of the volcano, which rose in a smooth line to the sky and from which a white pillar of smoke constantly arose. I asked Lao, the young man who acted as my guide, if he could get two or three of the men to climb the mountain with me. It could be done, there and back, in three days, I reckoned, and Skipper Johnny had promised to wait if I could get the carriers to go with me on the climb.

'No, Master,' Lao answered with a scared expression. 'No man go top side, no good, Master.' He would not even pass on my proposal to the other men.

I gave up and, instead, trained my camera on the young girls of the village who had put flowers in their hair and were dancing in a wide circle as an expression of pleasure at having visitors on the island. They laughed and swayed every time they passed us. They were not shy and apprehensive as so many native women are when white men visit their villages; they were self-assured, confident and free. Only when I pointed the film camera straight at them did they become a little hesitant and grave; but as soon as the camera had passed on, they were all smiles and laughter again. The women on the island were much more attractive than the men, who are of a slight build, with not very interesting faces. Most of the women, on the other hand, had fine expressive faces and strong, shapely bodies and they moved with the grace of gazelles. All they wore was a grass skirt which swayed as they walked to the rhythm of their bodies. The young girls wore only palm leaves, split long-ways around their hips; the men wore 'sporrans' of tapa bark or cotton fibre—and nothing else.

Some of the young men now began to join in the gaiety, beating the big village drums called *garamuts* with heavy sticks. The drums consisted of hollowed-out tree-trunks, about four feet long and eighteen inches deep, with carved heads of gods and magic figures on their sides. After half an hour or so the drumming and the singing and the dancing stopped, and most of the people resumed their daily routine which, as far as most of the men were concerned, was to sit dozing in the shade of the huts or repairing their nets and canoes on the beach.

By now Tom had had enough of chin tickling, so he swam back to the boat to have his afternoon nap. I, on the other hand, had become so fascinated by this little community living under the smouldering volcano that I spent the rest of my day wandering about with my camera, to catch pictures of their everyday life. In addition to a following of children, I had Lao with me to act as an ethnological dictionary. Here again, it was the women who did the hardest work. In a clearing behind the huts, they tilled the fields and grew such vegetables as yams, taro, spinach, pineapple and paw-paw melons. Bananas, coconuts and oranges grew wild in the jungle. The coconut shells were used as eating bowls, for there was no pottery. Round the huts were planted small bushes, producing a seed, which they used, pulverized, to dye their grass skirts and to decorate the magic masks which were kept in the big hut. I tried, in vain, to get hold of one of these ritual masks.

Unlike the tribes on New Guinea, the Manam islanders had no weapons at all; only fishing spears and a few bows and arrows for shooting birds. They were a happy people with no apparent anxieties and with an abundance of vegetables, fruit, game and fish. They had no desire to go on marauding raids and because of their isolation they had no cause to fear attacks from neighbours. This paradise island of Johnny's seemed ideal; there were no mosquitoes, no snakes, no crocodiles; though it was near the equator, the temperature was agreeable, thanks to the constant breeze from the ocean. I should have liked to settle down on the island for a while to study the little community's culture and habits, and to see how they compared with those of the more robust tribes on New Guinea. But there was no time; we were to sail the next morning.

I learned of a charming method the young men use on the island when they wish to summon their beloved. They hollow out a *gali* nut, which is triangular and about the size of a pipe, split it and make it into a kind of flute. With this simple instrument they contrive a gentle insinuating melody as they sit outside the girl's hut and wait for her at night. They often make beautiful carvings on these flutes. The children run wild on the island, carefree and happy. They learn to fend for themselves by following their mother about in the hut or the field and lending a happy hand now and then; they swim and dive and sail their small canoes from a tender age, and sometimes go fishing with the father.

Towards evening Skipper Johnny came paddling back in the canoe with two wild ducks which we had for supper with fried bananas and fresh fruit—all from the island of Manam. When at last I put out my sleeping-bag on the roof of the cabin, I saw a sight I shall never forget. It was a calm, warm night with half a moon and the Southern Cross decorating the sky. A little way down the coast the natives were going out, in twenty or thirty canoes, to harpoon fish by the light of big torches of dried palm leaves. When they had got a mile or two from the shore they spread out in a long line and turned back slowly towards the land, the flaming torches mirrored in the bright black water to attract the fish. In the bow of each canoe a native stood ready with a poised spear. The flying fish skimmed the water ahead of the canoes and left ribbons of phosphorescence behind them. Above the volcano the sky glowed with reflections from the interior of the crater; and from the shore I could hear, through the quiet night, the women chatting and singing as they waited for their men and the catch of fish.

16

I Meet a Danish Crocodile Hunter:
£25 for a Native: The River is Bewitched

EARLY next morning we raised anchor and set course
for the mouth of the Sepik river. Far out in the
ocean, before we made out the coastline hidden by a
heat mist, we met the brown, turbid water from the Sepik
river which stretched out like an enormous muddy tongue
far into the Bismarck Sea. The demarcation between
the deep blue sea and the muddy river is so clear that
one could swim with one's head in the river and one's legs
in the ocean. There were other signs to show that we were
nearing the mouth of the river: we passed several floating
islands of grass, borne along on the brown current into
the ocean. At midday we could see the surf on the bar
outside the river mouth, and after waiting an hour for
the tide we charged full speed into the river. The current
was unusually strong which meant that the rainy season
in the mountains, thousands of miles inland, had begun.
The river gradually narrowed to a width of about a mile,
but got deeper; on either side of its winding course were
vast swamps in which grew rushes and wild sugar-cane.
So devious was the river that sometimes we were sailing
north, sometimes south, east or west, but always against
the current. We kept near the shore, where the current

Up the muddy waters of the Sepik in suffocating heat

Big sister and baby brother

was least strong. After three or four hours the country began to change. The swamp gave way to stunted trees and thick bush, and later to sago palms and teak trees from which moss-covered lianas and other twining plants festooned towards the river. The jungle rose like a green wall from the brown water.

I had expected to see swarms of canoes manned by the sturdy Sepik natives; but during the whole afternoon, after passing a little village at the mouth of the estuary, we did not see a single canoe or native. Just before sunset, as Skipper Johnny had planned, we rounded a bend and caught sight of some buildings on a hill a little way back from the river. It was the Marienberg mission station and saw-mill where we were to spend the night. Marienberg is a Roman Catholic mission run by German missionaries, and it is also a well-organized business enterprise employing about eighty native boys who, under the supervision of the priests, fell the trees for timber.

We managed to get ashore and call on Father Bernadine and his four or five assistants before the sun went down and the noisy saw-mill stopped. As soon as the sun set, millions of mosquitoes came down on us from the jungle, but we pulled down the boat's capacious mosquito net and were soon asleep. Shortly before we left next morning we heard the noise of an aeroplane and soon after a small two-seater Auster came in sight and landed on a field behind the mission. It was the Roman Catholic Bishop Arkfeld from Wewak on a tour of inspection. He was alone in the plane, and I realized that he was the legendary Flying Bishop whom I had heard the pilots in Lae and Port Moresby discussing with great admiration. He was known as a fearless flyer who went up in all kinds of weather and who landed wherever there was a vestige of a clearing—often on the perilous slope of a hill. There were many stories about him among the pilots of New Guinea, a race not easily impressed. One of them, which he himself now confirmed, was of the time he flew a Government official, Fred Barron, out to Kairiru Island to inspect a mission school. The Auster plane touched down on a field mainly occupied by an enormous rock, and the Government official, sitting behind the pilot, thought his last hour had come; but the Bishop quickly flung open both the side doors and held them back with his arms so that they functioned as brake flaps! The plane stopped a few yards from the rock. The Bishop added that he still uses that method whenever he flies to Kairiru Island. Long after we had said good-bye to Marienberg, we could hear the whining noise from the saw-mills as we chug-chugged up-stream. Our next port of call was the Government Station at Angoram five or six miles further on and nearly a hundred miles from the mouth of the river.

Angoram, which also lies on a hillside, is the capital of the Sepik district. Here was the Government Station manned by a couple of officials; a few small saw-mills; a Chinese store; a Catholic mission—and a couple of resident crocodile hunters! There were ten Europeans and about a hundred and fifty natives employed at the mills. It was the last white outpost in this part of New Guinea, apart from a small station and a single officer another three hundred miles up-river. When we landed late in the afternoon, I had a pleasant surprise. One of the four or five Europeans who stood waiting to receive us called out to me in a broad Copenhagen dialect, 'Goddaw, Bjerre!' I looked up, surprised. When I jumped ashore and greeted him and the others, he told me his name was Flemming Carstensen. It turned out that we had been almost neighbours in Denmark.

'What are you doing here?' I asked him.

'Shooting crocodiles,' he answered. 'I knew you were on your way here. I heard it a few days ago on the radio.'

It was pleasant to hear Danish spoken again, but our time together was unfortunately far too short. Flemming Carstensen was just off up-river with an Australian companion to shoot crocodiles. I was to meet him again six weeks later, when we sailed together to Madang. Meanwhile, before we separated here in Angoram, he told me his story. After serving an agricultural apprenticeship he went to Australia to work on a big cattle farm; and when he had had enough of Australia he went to New Guinea as a plantation assistant at Coconut Products Ltd., a firm which owns thirty plantations on New Guinea, New Britain and the neighbouring islands. The firm soon made him plantation manager, and later gave him the job of transporting a thousand head of cattle from Australia to New Guinea to replace the animals killed off by the Japanese during the war. He had brought them over two hundred at a time and was now taking a couple of months holiday to shoot crocodiles on the Sepik.

They were a colourful and interesting collection of individualists here in Angoram, and I soon got to know them all. Apart from the two Government officials 'Sepik Robbie' and Jock McGregor, who had to wear shirts to keep their dignity among the natives, everyone else wore nothing but shorts and shoes. It was impossible to keep a shirt dry for more than five minutes. 'Sepik Robbie' was the senior official, a man in the early sixties, who had spent his life exploring the tributaries of the Sepik and taming head-hunters. He was humane and generous to all, black or white. He said himself that he had river water in his veins, thinned down with a drop of whisky, of course; and that he could not think of living anywhere else, even though the climate would doubtless curtail the years which

God had appointed for him. The other officer, Jock McGregor, was the fearless son of his famous father, one of New Guinea's pioneers, whose name was given to a range of mountains there.

Then there was Shanghai Brown, a very lovable original, also in the sixties, who had arrived there after a roving life in the Far East. Here, he said, he could get no farther from that civilization which he despised for its restraint and formality. He was an Englishman with an Oxford accent, and during the last war had served as a captain in the British fleet in the Far East. As he could not imagine himself continuing his career in an administrative office or as a docile pensioner, he had decided to shoot crocodiles on the Sepik river. That activity ensured him sufficient income so that he could live here without worries, in shorts and gym shoes. He had, moreover, virtually adopted seven or eight native children who looked up to him like a father.

The next type was Freddy Eickhorn who, like Shanghai and Robbie, was a part of Sepik itself. He was about forty, and had lived by the river for twenty-two years. He had come to Sepik with his father, a well-known German scientist, who settled down to research among the natives. Ten years ago, however, the father and two other white crocodile hunters had been attacked and killed by the natives in a village called Aibom, farther inland. Freddy escaped in the nick of time by swimming the river with his house-boy, and for eleven days they hid in a swamp, only their heads above the mud, until the murderous natives gave up looking for them. Freddy then took a canoe to a village further down the river where the natives looked after him and finally brought him to Angoram. Later he married the daughter of a chief, Salem, from one of the Sepik tributaries, Keram, and

set off in Freddy's boat with extra petrol for the long trip

The ceremonial house at Kambot

The village of Kambot on the Gorogoba river in the Sepik territory

became a white chief in her village. Now he owned one of the saw-mills in Angoram. We shall return to Freddy later. The next day I said good-bye to Skipper Johnny and to Tom, who sailed off towards the ocean and new adventures. Hospitable Jock McGregor put me up in the station guest hut, not realizing that there I had to share my bed and my table with a family of rats, who devoured everything not kept in tins and who ran across my legs during the night. A native prisoner, Laia, was allowed out of prison to act as my cook and house-boy. He was a peaceful and good-natured fellow, but nature had got the better of him while he was working in Madang. He had attacked a white woman; and now he had to pay for his crime by cooking for me.

I had decided to sail up one of Sepik's tributaries, where the natives were likely to be less influenced by civilization than those in the villages on the main river. I was keen to get off, but I soon learned not to push too hard in the Sepik climate. The problem was how to get transport in the smaller rivers. Freddy Eickhorn promised to sail me up the Keran river to his village and beyond that up a tributary where he promised I would find all I wanted in the way of the primitive. His motor boat, however, would not be returning for another week from a trip up the river where his men were marking trees for felling. I used the period of waiting to acclimatize myself. Because of constant and intense perspiration one had to drink all the time, but to avoid getting dysentery, one must either boil it or disinfect it with alcohol. The latter method was the only one known in Angoram . . . and that, naturally, left its mark on this charming little community. When a supply boat arrived, it always had a fair cargo of beer, gin, whisky and rum.

One day I had arranged with Shanghai Brown to go

with him in his canoe to a small village up-river to look for crocodiles. We had to start at sunrise to avoid the worst of the heat. When, at the first break of dawn, I came to his bungalow, I heard him making a great commotion. He was sitting on the edge of his bed, his eyes rolling, with a half-empty gin bottle in his horny hand.

'What's all this about?' I asked.

'It's all the fault of that little devil,' he said and pointed to one of his small boys, a fellow of ten or twelve who stood shyly, twisting his big toe on the floorboards and not quite sure whether to laugh or cry.

'I've got an oil fridge,' Shanghai continued. 'Every night that little fellow has to boil two pints of water and pour it into one of the many thousand empty gin bottles in the house and put it into the fridge. And every morning he has to bring me a bottle of ice water when I wake. He did that this morning, as usual. But when I had almost emptied the bottle, I realized that he brought me a bottle with gin in it instead of water. To hell with the little bastard!' Naturally, we did not hunt crocodiles that day.

Apart from his crocodile hunting, Shanghai was also employed to recruit natives for work in the plantations on the islands and along the coast. There is a constant shortage of native labour on these plantations, and several Europeans have made it their job to sail up and down the rivers of New Guinea recruiting young men in the villages for the plantations. They get from ten to twenty-five pounds per head, according to their transportation expenses. This may sound like slave traffic, but it is not, for the Government keeps a close eye on all recruiters. They must not, for instance, bribe the chiefs into forcing young men to go to the plantations. Recruiting must be on an absolutely voluntary basis. It has happened, though, that a slick recruiter has 'helped' natives to make up their minds when they have been in doubt about their inclinations! Before any of the recruits are sent to the plantations they must be inspected by the nearest Government official, whose duty it is to make clear the conditions of their employment. They are told that it is voluntary and they are told for how long and at what pay. All recruits are inspected by the Government doctor, who decides if they are fit to work. No plantation is allowed to recruit natives outside these conditions. The usual period of contract is eighteen months, after which it is the contractor's duty to transport the native back to his village. Most of them return to their homesteads, but some prefer to renew their contract and stay on the plantation. Those who return to remote and primitive villages are welcomed back as heroes. They bring strange presents with them; they win the admiration of the women as they boast of what they have seen and experienced. This rouses a certain envy among the other young men in the village so that the next time the recruiter comes up-river, new recruits are easily enrolled. In many cases the recruited natives are flown to the plantations, a cheaper method than keeping them in food for several days on a boat. It often happens that a young man from a village far inside the jungle will begin his journey to the plantations in a hollowed-out canoe, continue it in the recruiter's motor boat (a marvel he has never seen before) and complete it by plane. He travels from the Stone Age to the Air Age within a few weeks. Because of the emigration of young men many of the villages along the Sepik river are inhabited mainly by women, children and old men. When the plantation workers return they bring unfamiliar commodities back to the jungle; even in remote villages it is not uncommon nowadays to see cloth, pipes, mirrors and the like.

One evening during my stay in Angoram, I witnessed a

fantastic sight. The river suddenly seemed bewitched. A few inches above the surface of the water there appeared to be a waving carpet of white silk stretching from shore to shore up the river. Billions of white butterflies were hovering over the river and were reflected on its calm surface as though in a vast mirror. The natives dashed excitedly down to their canoes carrying their nets with them, paddled into the swarms of butterflies and in no time had netted masses of them. Some of the men, too, were spearing the fish that jumped to catch the insects. Within half an hour the carpet of white silk became thin and frayed as the butterflies gave up their death dance and were carried away by the stream. They live a very short time and before they die each year, just before the rainy season, they swarm over the river. The canoes come back with baskets full of dead butterflies, and the men set about grilling their catch over the village fires. Fried butterfly is the rarest delicacy they know.

17

A Climatic Hell: The Strange Jungle
Night: Life in a Village on Piles: The
Flying Dogs

A<small>T</small> last, one morning, Freddy Eickhorn's motor boat
came back. It was, to put it mildly, a comic sight
and looked as if it would fall to pieces any moment.
It had not seen paint for many years, great holes in the
hull and deck had been patched crudely with bits of tin
or timber. It was heavily overloaded with oil barrels and
sacks of sago, and some of the sacks had burst so that there
were pools of sago porridge all over the deck. 'It helps to
keep the deck waterproof,' said Freddy. But the vessel
could evidently float, and it was powered by a diesel
engine which, however, took us a couple of hours to start
next morning. But when at last we got going, we chugged
happily along through the muddy water of the Sepik,
towing behind us a couple of canoes with natives returning
to their villages further inland. Apart from ten boys from
the saw-mill, Freddy also took his wife, Salem, and his
four-year-old Albert along. The sun blazed down from a
cloudless sky and not a breath of wind stirred, so that the
temperature soon became like a Turkish bath. One's skin
burned and itched in the humid heat, and sweat poured
off us. The natives in the canoes sheltered under big palm
leaves with which they also fanned themselves. It was

unbearable in the cabin, so I rigged a sheet between the oil barrels on deck, where there was some breeze caused by the motion of the boat, although the sun reflected from the water burned one's eyes. Freddy and I became redder in the face all the time; the blood beat in one's temples, and I began to realize why the Sepik was called a climatic hell.

At midday we turned into the tributary, Keram, and sailed towards the south-east. The river, now less discoloured, turned and twisted, revealing one new and beautiful scene after the other. Long moss-covered lianas hung down to the water from the canopy of trees; large red flowers gleamed among the foliage. Some white birds called silk herons, I believe, startled by the sound of our motor, took flight and landed in the tree-tops from where they watched us with disapproving looks. Not until late afternoon, when the shadows fell across the river, did the temperature become bearable, and just before one more turning of the river we cast anchor and made fast to the shore. To prevent the boat from being rammed by drifting logs, the boys felled a small tree just in front of the boat so that the top of the tree fell outwards into the water, and then secured the lower part of the tree to the bank so as to provide a bulwark against drifting hazards. I now realized why there were so many patches on the sides of the boat.

The half-hour before dark was always the best time of the day. The heat was less oppressive, the blinding reflections of the sun disappeared, and the eerie silence which pervaded the jungle by day was now broken by the overture of the tropical night—the song of the cicada. It began with a few isolated chords which soon became multiplied by thousands. A few minutes later the birds joined in with whistles and warbles from birds of paradise and wood-pigeons. The concert lasted about half an hour and faded out into the cooing of pigeons as the night closed down upon the still river. Then came the mosquitoes, but luckily we had a large mosquito net which could be drawn completely over the boat's superstructure. Some of the natives built a small palm hut on shore and lit a couple of smoking fires to keep the insects off.

The final experience of the jungle night was the fascinating silent dance of the fire-flies among the trees. They floated like luminous sparks, in horizontal formation, and were switched on and off at regular intervals. After watching them for some time I could understand why soldiers were scared by the fire-flies in the jungle camps during the Pacific war. They mistook them for a stealthy Japanese attack!

As a fanfare to the birth of a new day came the first screeching of the birds, but the morning concert did not last long and it had none of the charm of the evening performance. After a burst of summoning notes, nature returned to silence again, the sun climbed quickly and the stupefying heat was on us again. Only the long-legged herons strutted philosophically by the shores. During the morning we passed a couple of canoes full of natives who shouted and waved at us, and an occasional field or settlement on the river shore. In the late afternoon we reached Freddy's village, Yip, and made fast to a raft by the shore. Women and children ran excitedly towards us when they saw the boat, for most of the twenty natives we had brought along with us were from this village, and many of them had been away a long time, so there was great rejoicing,

Salem, Freddy's wife, was also from here, and he himself was regarded as the chief of the village. He helped his subjects in many ways, imported new domestic animals, such as chickens, ducks and tame pigs, and furnished them with tools and utensils. In return the men worked for him, felling trees and making rafts. He had a lovely big bungalow in the middle of the village, built of palm trunks and bamboo, with doors and windows covered with mosquito nets, so that here at least we were safe from the bloodthirsty mosquitoes which increased in numbers and ferocity the further we came up the river. After two days here we continued up another tributary, Gorogoba, which runs into the Keram river, just near Freddy's village. The Gorogoba was only about fifty yards wide, and its water, clear as crystal, mirrored the green jungle which towered towards the sky on either side of us. After four or five hours during which we passed several canoes, we at last reached our goal, a large village called Kambot which stretched for half a mile on each side of the river, and possessed a couple of hundred inhabitants. Freddy was again welcomed like a home-coming millionaire uncle from the States. We settled down in a grass hut for the three weeks ahead, so that I could take films of this village on piles, a settlement typical of many along the Sepik tributaries.

The houses were built in a row facing the river, on massive stakes two or three yards above the ground, and were considerably larger than the houses in which the tribes of the interior lived. They were made of palm trunks and bamboo and thatched with rush and palm leaves. Over some of the large houses the roofs were built in a sloping triangle which projected far over the gables at either end. Only a few houses had window openings. The reason for pile building was that the river rises above its banks during the rainy season and floods large areas on either side. The villagers are then safe in their perches and can wade back and forth to their houses.

In the middle of the village, on one bank, was a huge

ceremonial house, the *tamburan* house. It was a colossal building which must have required considerable teamwork, ingenuity and planning. The floor was based on big tree trunks, five yards above the ground; the building itself was fifty yards long and fifteen wide. Under the triangular gable of the roof, which faced the river, was painted an immense god, which represented the spirits of the forefathers and stood guard over the villagers when they gathered in the ceremonial house. It was particularly during the rainy season, when outdoor work was stopped, that they gathered here, sometimes for ritual dancing and feasts. The biggest dance took place at New Year, in the middle of the rainy season, and lasted for several days. This temple alone indicated that the Sepik natives possess a more advanced culture than the Kukukukus. With the exception of some of the children, they had all seen Europeans before and there was therefore no difficulty for me in making a film of their everyday life.

For the next couple of weeks I went about with Freddy or one of his boys as interpreter; we walked about the village or sailed with the natives to their fields and fishing beats. Their dress was a minimum: the men wore a bit of bark in front, the women wore colourful grass skirts. The women here did not seem subdued or oppressed by the men, yet they were certainly the ones who worked hardest. The men took things easily and devoted much time to discussing the affairs of the village. Nevertheless, they put in more time in the fields than I had seen natives do anywhere else in New Guinea—possibly because all the clearing, sowing and harvesting had to be done between two rainy seasons. The fields are often far away from the villages, as they never use the same field two years running. The favourite crop was sweet potatoes; next came taro, cucumbers, spinach, pumpkins, water melons and sugar-cane. Coconuts and bananas grow abundantly in the jungle. Their basic food, however, is sago, which is made from the starchy marrow of the sago palm. The production of the sago is a laborious process. The men fell the trees and cut the trunks into suitable lengths; the women do the rest. They hack the marrow out of the trunks with a wooden chopper and then pulverize the pulp until it looks like sawdust. The next process takes place on a small raft by the river bank. Here the sawdust is put in a large funnel made of palm leaves and water is poured over it. The water, which absorbs the sago starch, is collected in a bark vessel in which it stays over-night until the starch sinks to the bottom. This is then scraped away and boiled down in a large clay container to the consistency of a very sticky jelly. The sago is finally wrapped in green abanana palm leaves in convenient sizes for the larder. Sago porridge twice a day all the year round! They eat it both hot and cold. I tried it myself, but was relieved to know that I had other possibilities of satisfying my hunger. It is undoubtedly a nourishing food, for the Sepik people have fine physiques. They did not seem to suffer from malaria probably because they get immunity with their mother's milk. On the other hand, many of them suffered from ring-worm. The preparation of the sago is a co-operative task. Several women from different families work together to supply the village with its daily ration of sago, or 'sak sak', as they call it.

The women made most of the domestic tools. They plaited raffia for fishing nets and made fish traps from the fibre of palm leaves, and large clay jars hardened by fire. The men performed the heavier tasks such as building and repairing the houses and fashioning canoes from hollowed-out tree-trunks. There were canoes of many sizes; tiny ones for the children and long-distance canoes to hold as many as ten or fifteen men. The men always stood when they paddled, the women always sat. Most of the canoes were decorated with painted heads of crocodiles on the bow. The Sepik people had more sense of decoration than most other tribes in New Guinea. The men carved large images for the festive hall, and the women dyed their skirts in striped patterns, and decorated their clay jars. Most of the decoration was done during the long idle hours in the rainy season.

In spite of the climate the natives were surprisingly full of energy. The women especially were active from sunrise to nightfall, for it was important to gather enough food for the rainy season. When they did pause for a short rest, they fanned themselves with little rice leaf fans to keep the mosquitoes away. Many of the natives slept at night in large, oblong baskets or inside mats shut in at each end, to keep the bloodsuckers away. I myself had only enough energy to work a few hours in the morning and again in the late afternoon. During the hottest hours, in the middle of the day, I slept or gasped for breath under the mosquito net. The heat grew more and more oppressive as the rainy season drew nearer; the sky was frequently clouded and the first light showers began to fall during the night. I developed the fancy that each drop of rain produced one more mosquito. They were by now so innumerable and persistent as to sit on one's spoon during a meal. Some of the natives daubed themselves in mud as a protection against the pests.

Another sign that the rainy season was near were the mists that came down on the river at night. A new nightly visitor now appeared—horrible creatures called 'flying dogs', which were really outsize bats. These were revolting creatures, with pointed hooks on their black wings and a general prehistoric appearance, which raided the wild bananas in the jungle by night and sometimes even swarmed into the villages in search of food. In the day-time they slept, head downwards, in dark places in the jungle. One day there was a great commotion behind one of the huts in the village. The natives had caught a six-foot boa constrictor about to attack a group of young pigs, and were beating it with heavy sticks across the neck in order to stupefy and paralyse it. The snake struggled furiously to get away, but they managed to cripple it sufficiently to seize it round the neck and finish it off. They devoured this primitive speciality and carefully kept the skin to make covers for their ceremonial drums.

The flying dogs inspired the children to perform a funny game for me, in which only the boys took part. One boy stood with his arms raised, representing a banana tree; two others then came hopping towards him, uttering the piercing cries of the flying dogs. They circled round the banana tree and then flew back to the other flying dogs and told them about the bananas. Then the whole swarm of them, barking and screaming, flung themselves upon the poor 'banana tree'. But now there appeared on the scene a boy who was the owner of the banana tree, carrying in his hand a big branch, with which he beat the flying dogs. Every time he scored a hit on one of them, the victim had to fall down. At last he had killed the lot and, with a jubilant cry of victory, the whole game broke up in laughter. They would play the same game over and over again like a flock of happy boys on a playground at home.

As long as the recorder was a novelty to the natives, it was easy for me to get them to demonstrate some of their ceremonial dances for me, in full panoply, with songs and music on drums and flutes. Apart from the ritual dances they had others to celebrate everyday occurrences, such as the launching of a new canoe or moving into a new hut.

They had erotic dances, too, with songs lamentably unsuitable for translation. While I was recording their songs they would often improvise new ones about each other, to everybody's great amusement. One day one of the dancers sang a song which won hearty approval. In his song he revealed the suspicion that his wife had been unfaithful to him, and he proceeded to enumerate her faults without, however, mentioning her name. But the woman, far from hiding her head in shame, revenged herself by improvising a song in which she criticized her her lover and related how she had fooled him. I was told that the custom of exchanging wives for a night or two was quite common in the Sepik villages

18

A Nocturnal Crocodile Hunt

THERE are crocodiles in all the shallow rivers of New Guinea. Because of the unfortunate episode with Shanghai Brown's gin bottle, I had been cheated of a crocodile hunt in Angoram, but now I made up for it. Armed with Freddy's rifle I went out a couple of evenings with some of the natives to shoot *puk puk*, as they call the crocodile. Just before sunset we started off; eight men in two large canoes, which we had lashed together in the optimistic expectation that we should need a large transport for our 'bag'. During the day-time it was difficult to catch them, but at night with the help of long torches (or a strong electric torch) it was easier. It was a quiet evening with no wind and some cloud, ideal for crocodile hunting. We paddled a mile or two up-river to a swamp with tall sugar-cane and river grass on either bank. It was now almost dark. I sat in front of one of the canoes with my rifle and an electric torch, and in the stern of the other canoe sat Freddy's house-boy with a torch and a harpoon ten feet long made fast to a strong rope. We went close into the bank and paddled slowly among the rushes for about an hour.

There are two ways of hunting crocodile by night. You

can camouflage your canoe in the swamp and lure the animals by imitating their noises; or you can drift silently with the stream, letting your torch play over the surface of the water. In either case, absolute quiet is essential. We combined the two methods of alternatively drifting and lying in wait. First, we carefully backed the canoes into the rushes and switched off our electric torches, and also took the precaution to rub mosquito repellent on our faces and hands. For the first ten minutes we sat absolutely quiet and listening intently. The only noise we could hear was the buzz of the mosquitoes and the quiet murmur of the water. Then one of the paddlers behind me started, every thirty seconds, to copy the cry of the female crocodile, a quiet 'Wuk, wuk, wuk,' like the sound of a hollow reed.

After each call we listened for any sign of movement in the rushes. I had my rifle at the ready and the boy had his harpoon poised. Suddenly I felt a slight swaying of the canoe as the boss-boy got up, raised his harpoon and stared up the river. In a gleam of pale moonlight we saw a dark shadow moving slowly towards us. The paddler kept up his call, I raised my rifle and waited for a signal from the boss-boy. But at that moment he flashed his torch on to the gliding shadow and snorted 'A log!' There was a sigh of disappointment from all the men. We then decided to drift down the river and search the banks. Checking the canoes with the paddles so as not to drift too quickly we floated along ten yards from the bank, playing our torches all the time. We had gone a few hundred yards down the river when we observed in the light of the torches two small red dots just above the surface of the water.

'*Puk, puk*, true, Master,' the boss-boy whispered.

Very slowly the paddlers swung the canoe round and closed in upon the two red spots. The boss-boy kept his light on them and again raised his harpoon in his right hand. Holding my breath, I noticed how the distance grew less and less. I recalled the tip Shanghai Brown had given me: 'Shoot between the eyes. If you are far off, shoot a little below them, and if you are near, a tiny bit above them. And keep your hands inside the boat. If you fall overboard and get caught by the crocodile and pulled down, don't struggle; he will only try to get a better grip on you with his teeth. Try to find its eyes and press your thumbs into them. Then he will let go at once.' It sounded very simple!

We were now only a few feet from the red spots. The boss-boy gave the signal, a clucking sound with his tongue, and I pressed the trigger at the same moment as he hurled his harpoon—not so much to kill the beast, but to prevent it sinking. My shot had hit the right spot, for the crocodile was dead when we hauled it into the canoe by the harpoon line. To make quite sure, though, the paddlers bound its jaws together, before they pulled it in. They had had their experiences. It was a little fellow, only four feet long. We now relaxed a little. We were tired and stiff from sitting still so long, so we went ashore to stretch our legs for twenty minutes and then resumed the drift down river again.

At midnight, after a couple of hours vain searching, we decided to return to Kambot. But a little above the village our luck turned, and we almost ran into a couple of red crocodile eyes exactly ahead of us. We were now using only one torch to mark the way, and I was dozing with fatigue, when the boss-boy gave me a nudge. I saw the two red spots, but before I could collect my wits to aim and fire, the boss-boy let go with his harpoon just as the crocodile started a crash dive. The harpoon struck and the boss-boy got the animal alongside the canoe. It was not a big one, but it was fighting furiously to shake out

A snake held like this can neither bite nor escape

Kambot women plaiting a fishing basket

Making the clay pots for cooking sago

the harpoon which had penetrated one side of its neck. The jaws were writhing with a horrible snapping sound, the tail beat the water and the side of the canoe. At last one of the paddlers got a thin bamboo line round its jaws, and the man hauled it aboard immediately, tying its legs as well. Not one of the natives spoke during the battle; they all knew exactly what to do and did it coolly. We were at Kambot before the crocodile died. A few evenings later we bagged another pair, the smaller of which was only a yard long. We saw several larger specimens, but they were apparently wary of lights in the night and vanished quickly.

The natives enjoyed the meat the next day, and even to my taste it was not too bad. I salted a couple of the skins and took them back with me to Denmark. I had difficulty later in getting them properly tanned. In Sydney I was told it would take four months. Then I took them to London where I was told they could best be done in Brussels. I finally got them done for me in Valby (Denmark) in a fortnight. I pass this information on to anyone else who may be thinking of hunting crocodiles.

19

The Vailala Madness: Ships from Heaven

A**T** last the rain came: not like the Indian monsoon which arrives on the dot each year and sets in at full strength, but after many preliminary warnings of its imminence. First there was rain during the nights; then in the afternoons, and finally after a while in the mornings as well, though as a rule there were a few dry hours in the middle of the day. 'The rain hasn't really started yet,' said Freddy. 'Wait about a week, then it *will* rain.' The first rains were welcome for they cooled the air. Earlier on we had gone to sleep exhausted immediately after supper; now we were able to sit up for hours, under the mosquito net on the veranda, and talk far into the night. In these sessions our talk ranged widely: about the circular saw Freddy needed for his saw-mill, about his secret dream to go once on an ocean liner to Europe, to the homeland he had left as a boy. Every year he flew down to Brisbane in Australia, where his daughter went to school, but he could not imagine living long in civilization. When he was away he always longed for the river, which had become the home where he had lived for so many years with Salem and his three children. His eldest son, Bill, had trained as a teacher and was teaching in a Government school for native children.

We discussed the habits and beliefs of the natives. 'We never get to know them completely,' said Freddy. 'Look at our friends here in Kambot, where life goes on peacefully and harmoniously. Yet even after long and friendly contact with Europeans, a sort of primitive volcanic eruption can break out among the natives. Only a few years ago forty of them lost their heads in the Ambunti district a little further up the river. They were attacked by another tribe who had an old account to settle. All had seemed peaceful enough in the district—yet suddenly this massacre was committed. A few years ago these people were head-hunters. They are not any more. Their old habits and ceremonies are slowly disappearing—and leaving a dangerous vacuum. When you take something away from these people you ought to replace it. But how? You cannot just give them a ready-made religion to follow. We understand very little of their psychology, which is so very different from ours.

'A few years ago we saw this vacuum in operation. A sort of holy war broke out among the natives, a mass hysteria which spread like wild-fire through great areas of New Guinea. The movement was directed against the Europeans, and if it hadn't been checked in time would have had bloody results. As it was there were many ugly incidents. The significant thing about it was that it flared up not among the primitive natives of the jungle, but among the natives around the plantations and mission stations, and it only affected tribes in contact with Europeans. Most of the natives around here were in contact with the mission station and had heard sermons about Christianity. But you can't suddenly change a people's mentality. The natives tried, more or less, to adapt their beliefs to the new Christian doctrines and drew some queer conclusions in the attempt. When told that we rise from the dead, and that in Heaven all are equal, the natives inferred that all who died would be born again—*with a white skin*. And from then on they believed that all white people were reincarnated natives: in other words their forefathers returned in a new guise. What is more, they were now persuaded that all the white people's goods were really presents the spirits in Heaven had entrusted to the whites to deliver to the natives. The whites had stolen these goods, and were holding them in warehouses and shops and forcing the natives to work and pay for the goods that were rightly theirs already!

'They wanted these goods, and as they couldn't see any direct way of getting at them, they turned towards their traditional superstitions. By the help of magic rites they would implore their forefathers' spirits in Heaven to send the goods to them direct by ship or plane. The more they talked about it, the more they persuaded themselves that this was how it could be made to happen! They gradually worked themselves up to a frenzy of grievance, and the movement spread to other villages along the coast. Some places they laid a "welcome" table ready for the fore-fathers' spirits to come along with all the goods they wanted. It was a *white* man's table they laid; with white tablecloth, tin plates and white man's dishes.

'The rumour spread that a big ship was on the way to them from the spirits in Heaven, fully loaded with tobacco, cloth, preserves, electric torches, knives, axes; and with rifles and ammunition too, it was said later. The weapons were to drive the whites out of the country, so that they couldn't steal any more of the goods that were intended for the people. Some dark night or other the natives would imagine they saw a ship nearing the village from the sea. They would run out of their huts, swing burning torches and shout and scream in hysterical excitement. They

Sepik woman with sago on a palm leaf plate

Kambot chief in full ritual dress

completely lost their mental balance and these fevers of hysteria could last for several weeks, even months. The whole rhythm of the daily life of the village was disturbed, the fields went untended (for now it was not necessary to work in them any more, for all they needed was on the way). In some places they even started to build large huts to store the goods when the ship arrived. In the huts they put stones, sticks and piles of leaves as symbols of the guns and goods they expected.

'The oddest thing was that this madness in many cases resulted in hysterical attacks of cramp. When they were seized by their delusions, their bodies would shiver, they swung their arms violently about and shook their heads madly, finally falling down and writhing in pain while the froth poured from their mouths. Some got the "gift of tongues" and shouted a lot of gibberish, which no one could understand. It was believed that the spirits were talking.

'This delirium was contagious. If one man was taken with cramps, the whole village would soon have them, too. Some of them took up fantastic postures, others improvised crazy dances and songs, the latter being sometimes a corruption of the hymns they had learned at the mission schools. Even peaceful mission boys, who the missionaries thought were quite Christian, ran amok in this way.'

When Freddy told me these things, I recalled an odd experience I had had when I lived with Barry Osborne in Nondugl. Once we were awakened at two o'clock in the morning by an excited boss-boy, who knocked on the bedroom door and told Barry some confused nonsense, which I didn't quite catch in my sleepy state. But I wakened quickly enough when I saw Barry jump out of bed, put on his trousers and run out into the dark. I hurried after him and the boss-boy over to the boys' huts. Here all was wild confusion. Four of the boys were trying to hold down a boy who kicked and shouted wildly, his lips frothing, his eyes wild and empty. We tied him up, and Barry gave him a sedative injection. Barry called it momentary madness, and said, that it was not unusual for some of the natives at the post to get such an attack. The next day the boy was kept in bed and was given one more injection, but on the third day he was working normally.

Freddy continued, while the rain drummed on the roof:

'To start with none of the Europeans were aware of what was going on inside the heads of the confused natives, but it gradually dawned on them that something was very wrong. The plantation owners along the coast, where the movement spread most, felt their lives threatened, and the authorities at Port Moresby intervened. The worst fanatics were removed and the "warehouses", that were waiting for the goods, were burned.'

The *Vailala* madness, as it is called, is under control on the Papua coast, but it had spread like a wave over New Guinea and up to a few years ago it would break out here and there, in the Highlands as well as among the tribes on the north coast. In some places it developed into tragedies. At one place on the north coast, near Bogia, the natives burned down their own huts, ruined their fields, slaughtered their pigs and sat for several days on the beach waiting for the ship with their forefathers' spirits to arrive with food for them. The movement took various forms in different places according to what the natives could imagine and according to the rumours they heard. The authorities did not call it Vailala madness any more, but the cargo-cult: it was always about cargoes from Heaven.

In the 'thirties many of the natives in the Central Highlands heard, for the first time, the far-away sound of an aeroplane. They were frightened. What could the noise possibly be? Was it an earthquake, or the sound of distant floods? Or was it the sound of a large bird of prey? The noise went on and soon they saw a large, shiny bird—an aeroplane. They threw themselves to the ground in terror and dared not look up for fear of being killed if the birds should see them. When the terrifying sound at last faded behind the mountains they rose and looked around. They agreed that something must be done to protect themselves against this huge and doubtless predatory bird. So they melted some pig's fat and poured it out over the soil as an offering to the spirits of their forefathers. Then they took some leaves which had a protective power and tied them in their hair and over their burdens to protect them against the bird's deadly magic. Time passed, and other aeroplanes were seen and heard. From the northerly Kamano district, where a new station had just been opened, came some strange rumours. It was said that the flying object was called 'The bird of the heavenly mother' and that it carried many white men in its belly which were dropped out when it touched the ground. Slowly they got accustomed to the bird, but they were still afraid of it. Yet, as it did not seem to hurt anybody, they began to think they were mistaken about its evil power. They wondered a lot who these men were and where they came from. Since they came from Heaven they must be heavenly beings.

Then natives were familiar with many stories about the heavenly world, and about the people from Heaven who visit the earth: people (said the myths) who were white because they had been so near to the sun. The white men were powerful beings, who could rule lightning and thunder and all the elements of the world. They came from Anabaga—the world of the dead; they were their forefathers' spirits sent back to life again by the two great spirits of their myths: Jugumishanta and Morofonu. It all seemed to make sense for a primitive brain.

Fear of the unknown dominated their imagination. As the natives around the new post at Kainantu in the Highlands gradually got used to the sight of the white men, they used their new-found knowledge about him to impress and overawe their more ignorant neighbours, who themselves had not seen these strangers. The rumours spread widely, like rings when a stone is thrown into water, and as the stories passed from mouth to mouth, from village to village and from tribe to tribe, they became more and more far-fetched. One rumour disseminated from Kamano was that, when the white men came, all pregnant women would die; they would be killed by snakes which the white men would bring along and which would penetrate their wombs and cause death. To prevent this, the husbands of the pregnant women made aprons of bark which they tied round the waists of their wives to conceal the fact that they were pregnant. To make doubly sure they fitted them out with bark napkins. Some of the women got so worked up with terror that they aborted the unborn child to save their own lives. In some of the villages the men built a large hut capable of holding all the inhabitants. They collected a large supply of food and water and all of them, men, women and children barred themselves inside the hut.

The men carried out various rites: one was to chew a flower called *Oggona* and spit it out on the pregnant woman's body to counteract the venom of the 'snakes'. The men kept watch during the night, while the women slept. Another magic they employed was to slaughter several pigs and spray the blood over the bellies of the pregnant women and over the threshold of the hut. The idea was to deceive the snakes into believing that the women had already been killed. They kept this up for some days, but there was no sign of the 'snakes' nor of the evil spirit *Katokkatoveifani*, who was supposed to accompany them; so they decided to leave the hut, now believing that the rumours from Kamano must be false. When they left the hut, however, they killed some more pigs and sprayed more blood upon the women.

Shortly afterwards a man came back from Kamano with the news that the spirits of the dead, that is to say the white men, would give sea-shells and other riches to their friends and relations. This tale, of course, was based on the fact that the Europeans at the Kainantu post gave the neighbouring natives sea-shells, knives, axes, empty food tins, tobacco, cloth and salt in exchange for pigs and produce from the fields. The natives assumed, however, that these gifts were the rewards of those who had observed the proper ceremonies for the dead. More and more rumours arrived from Kainantu, where the natives kept on getting presents in exchange for food. Some of the presents were subsequently traded from village to village and afforded visible proof that the stories were true. But because these 'presents' trickled through into the interior on such a scanty scale the natives concluded that the spirits, in the shape of the white men, were angry with them, so they went through various rituals to appease the visitants. But as only an occasional knife or a few sea-shells arrived, they believed that the Europeans were deliberately with-holding the presents which the forefathers' spirits in Heaven had sent them. The belief that the white men were their reincarnated forefathers remained unshaken, but when the natives did not get the presents they expected, they turned against them. The confusion into which the primitive mind is thrown by the impact of white civilization was revealed by another widespread native movement which developed in 1940 among the natives around the Markham valley of Northern New Guinea, who had been under the influence of the missionaries. The natives in the villages of Tampir, Mirir, Omisuan, Wampur and Arau built themselves some huts which they called 'wireless houses' through which, they imagined, they would receive messages from the tribes along the Markham river. The huts had little poles on their roofs, a pitiful imitation of the radio masts on the Government posts. The natives used to assemble these huts and do military exercises with sticks for rifles. They believed that Jesus was to arrive soon, and that the news of his arrival would be received at the 'radio huts'. They were learning how to use rifles for, they said, when Jesus came he would help them all to get the real weapons so that they could throw the whites out of the country. In the village of Wampur there was a different prophecy. The sticks with which they were doing their exercises would be turned into torches when Jesus came, and when the torches were burned down they would all wake up in Heaven.

When the authorities heard of these goings-on they told the natives that the Government would, of course, be advised of Jesus's arrival and would pass the news on. This handling of the situation quietened the natives; but a year later another manifestation developed. The natives in the village of Omisuan heard rumours that their fore-fathers' spirits in Heaven had sent them a large supply of goods. It was the usual story—that the white men in Lae had kept the goods back in order to force the natives to work. But the spirits had discovered this trick and were themselves coming down to earth to distribute the presents. The natives, therefore, deserted their fields and let their food rot. One of the men, a former plantation boy, was appointed as go-between between the spirits and the village, and took up residence in a 'radio hut'. The inhabitants anointed themselves with oil sent them by the Markham River natives which, they believed, would help them to turn their black skins white, and ensure that they would receive the same goods as the white men got.

Such were the delusions the poor primitives developed from the well-meaning efforts of the missionaries to care for their black souls. The villages of Omisuan and Arau, especially, had been under the influence both of Lutheran and Adventist Evangelists, whose talk of Doomsday and the Second Coming had become inextricably muddled with the mythology and beliefs of these hapless pagans and had produced a religio-political ferment among their numbers. These spiritual crises have occurred during the last twenty years among many other primitive people in New Zealand, the Fiji Islands, Java, the Celebes, the Solomon Islands and, especially, in Africa. The Mau Mau movement in Africa originated in a confused magic which took a political turn when ex-service tribesmen organized a military rising. The Australian authorities in New Guinea have realized that governing a primitive people involves a sympathetic insight into their minds. Australian anthropologists and psychologists have been assigned to study and analyse the various 'movements' among the natives, and nowadays all officials posted to New Guinea have to go through a course of anthropology at the University of Sydney. The white man has brought peace to the cannibal tribes of New Guinea, but he did not at first realize the high price paid for this peace in terms of the disruption of the native's ancient way of life.

20

Duck Hunt: The Bloodsucking Leeches: Two White Officials Murdered by the Natives: Malaria

IT is impossible to write about New Guinea without mentioning rain: noisy, splashing rain, rain that quietly pours down, rain that just hangs in the damp air and makes everything drip. Rain day and night. It rained through the roof in the bungalow in Kambot, so we had to put the tarpaulin over the mosquito net. Outside, the Gorogoba river overflowed its banks and turned the ground into mud. Freddy and I wanted to return to Angoram; but some of his boys had taken the motor boat down to Yip on the Keram river to fell teak trees for rafting down to the saw-mill in Angoram. We expected them back every day to fetch us, and Freddy was getting worried that something might have happened to them. It was depressing to sit doing nothing, listening to the drip and splash of the rain, so we decided to paddle up to a swamp with some natives and shoot wild duck.

We started off in four canoes, with ten men from Kambot who poled and paddled almost a whole day through the rushes, for in the middle of the river the current was too strong. At last we reached a small village of about ten huts on stilts. The ground was completely flooded, but their pigs and other possessions were safely stowed on

In the rainy season the natives sit in the big communal hut and fan themselves to keep the mosquitoes off

The white mask in the ceremonial house symbolizes the spirits of their forefathers

Canoeing on the Gorogoba river

platforms under the huts immediately above the surface of the water. It was rather late in the day and we were soaked through, but we decided to paddle a little farther into the swamp, with some of the natives from the village, to see if we could find any duck. And we did. Twice we came upon a covey of them. The natives flung javelins at them and then jumped overboard to recover the birds whose wings they had broken or which they had stunned. They bagged a brace for us in this way, whereas Freddy only got one with his rifle. A triumph for the primitive!

For a change there were only showers that day. The rain ran off the natives' sweaty bodies at once. We, on the other hand, sat with our soaking shirts sticking to our backs, but we had to keep them on as a defence against the mosquitoes who came out as soon as each shower was over. At one place, where we paddled through water only knee-high, I got out to stretch my legs, but within thirty seconds they were covered with blood-sucking leeches, so I quickly got back in the canoe. Their bite is not painful, but one has to be careful not to tear them off or their heads remain behind and poison the wound. My remedy was to light a cigarette and press it on to their tails, on which they promptly fell off.

During the night we slept on mats in a hut in a small village where we were able to dry out our soaked clothes. Next morning we paddled back to Kambot in pouring rain, down-stream now, and tearing at speed between drifting tree-trunks and drifting islands of grass. When we neared the village we looked out eagerly to see if Freddy's boat had arrived. There it was, moored to the raft, and we both sighed with relief. I was afraid of any further delay in getting my precious films away to be developed. I kept them in big tin boxes with the necessary chemicals, and these were running out.

We packed our things as quickly as possible, and that night we got to Yip. Next morning we continued full speed with the current and reached Angoram before night-fall, when we found the whole colony in a wild commotion: news had just come by radio that two Australian officials, Szarka and Harris, had been killed by the natives. They had been patrolling the south-west area of the Sepik district and had been lured from their huts by some natives offering to sell them some vegetables, and while bending down to examine the vegetables they had been clubbed, dragged into the jungle and killed in the most bestial way. A native policeman who had been with them had also been attacked and wounded, but had managed to escape to the nearest mission from which the news of the attack had reached the authorities. The District Commissioner in Wewak, Mr Timberley, arrived the next day with a transport plane to collect reinforcements of native police in Angoram; and at the same time my permission to continue up into the back country was cancelled, for reasons of safety. But I had no desire to stay any longer on the Sepik. I was now reaching the end of my resources, I had no more films and chemicals and, in spite of daily doses of paludrin tablets, the malaria was getting the better of me. Four days later I went with the supply boat to Madang, dizzy with headache and fever.

21

In Hospital in Madang

THE blood is throbbing in my temples, there is a buzzing in my ears, brought on by the daily dose of 25 milligrams of quinine. I am only vaguely aware that sheets are changed and that sweat is washed off my face and arms. The air is stifling, heavy: if only the ventilators in the ceiling could go a bit faster. In between the attacks of fever I listen for the footstep of the orderly.

'Boy, bring me more water.'

The nurses smile at me and their encouraging words are like ointment on an open wound. In the evening the fever breaks out again. I can feel it coming on: the rapid beat of the pulse, the intensified pain in the head. I try to tear the sheets, but there is no strength in my hands; I cannot lift them from the sheet. I want to scream in despair, but sink into dark fantasies. My spirit leaves me and wanders around: sits in the stern of a canoe to protect the paddler and secure his catch; flies into the mountains and sits on a branch of a tree with all the other spirits; tears down into a village and stones a prisoner to death while the whole village screams with approval. It runs off with Moma-kowa, who swings his club and spreads death and terror; it lurks in the dark shadows and lures the Kumans into the Highland swamps; it falls into an abyss because Angu cannot hold on to my foot any longer and while I disappear over the edge, he is shouting into my ear: 'Okay Master, Okay Master.'

On and on my spirit gyrates in a mad ecstasy. Now it is standing on the Vailala beach shouting: 'The ship is coming, the ship is coming.' Then it is swept off to a magic ritual in a moonlit jungle. 'Ingiham,' I shout, 'What does the spirit look like?' He shakes his head and says, 'But Master, it does not *look:* it is.'

'Nonsense, Inghiham,' I shout, 'Answer me———'

'Quiet, quiet, please.' The nurse wipes my forehead and gently pushes me back on to my pillow. I am given an injection and a dry sheet is spread under me. For a few moments I lie and stare at the night-light, and listen to the heavy breathing next to me. Then I discover that the pain in my head has gone; next the spirit leaves me again and I fall into a heavy sleep.

Next day the doctor, having heard of my attack says, 'We had better stop giving Mr Dane the big doses now. Only two capsules a day, and no more injections.' The fever has burnt itself out, and now I progress day by day. I lie and listen to the sounds: a dog barks, a door is banged. I hear a quiet conversation between two English women. A car drives slowly up to the hospital, gravel crunching under the wheels. It stops, and the motor gently ticks over. All the familiar sounds from the world I belong to. As I lie there I decide I shall spend a week in the cool mountains before, after a year's absence, I start my journey home. Once more I shall feel the clean air in my lungs, watch the colours of the sunset, and hear the calls of the carriers echoing over the green valleys. I shall walk alone in the mountains and feel at one with all the elements of nature. I shall sense the rhythm of all created life.